The Aztecs: A Very Short Introduction

VERY SHORT INTRODUCTIONS are for anyone wanting a stimulating and accessible way in to a new subject. They are written by experts and have been published in more than 25 languages worldwide.

The series began in 1995, and now represents a wide variety of topics in history, philosophy, religion, science, and the humanities. The VSI library now contains 300 volumes—a Very Short Introduction to everything from ancient Egypt and Indian philosophy to conceptual art and cosmology—and will continue to grow in a variety of disciplines.

Very Short Introductions available now:

For more information visit our web site
www.oup.com/vsi/

Davíd Carrasco

THE AZTECS

A Very Short Introduction

OXFORD
UNIVERSITY PRESS

OXFORD
UNIVERSITY PRESS

Oxford University Press, Inc., publishes works that further
Oxford University's objective of excellence
in research, scholarship, and education.

Oxford New York

Auckland Cape Town Dar es Salaam Hong Kong Karachi
Kuala Lumpur Madrid Melbourne Mexico City Nairobi
New Delhi Shanghai Taipei Toronto

With offices in

Argentina Austria Brazil Chile Czech Republic France Greece
Guatemala Hungary Italy Japan Poland Portugal Singapore
South Korea Switzerland Thailand Turkey Ukraine Vietnam

Copyright © 2012 by Davíd Carrasco

Published by Oxford University Press, Inc.
198 Madison Avenue, New York, NY 10016

www.oup.com

Oxford is a registered trademark of Oxford University Press

Library of Congress Cataloging-in-Publication Data
Carrasco, Davíd.
The Aztecs : a very short introduction / Davíd Carrasco.
p. cm. — (Very short introductions)
Includes bibliographical references and index.
ISBN 978-0-19-537938-9 (pbk.)
1. Aztecs. I. Title.
F1219.73.C354 2011
972—dc23
2011025597

1 3 5 7 9 8 6 4 2

Printed in Great Britain
by Ashford Colour Press Ltd., Gosport, Hants.
on acid-free paper

To the archaeologists who excavate the Great Aztec Temple and to Friedrich Katz, who first taught me about Aztec civilization

717

Contents

List of illustrations

Preface

Writing a Very Short Introduction to the Aztecs includes
a long journey back through the more than two-thousand-year
history of the rise of urban life that they inherited and
reformulated between 1300 and 1521 CE. It involves
adjustments in the use of the popular names "Aztec" and
"Montezuma," names that the population who lived in and in
relation to the city of Tenochtitlan never used. "Aztec" is a
Nahuatl-derived term meaning "people from Aztlan," the
revered place of origin of the various ethnic groups who
eventually dominated central Mesoamerica in the century
before the arrival of Europeans. The people we call Aztecs,
however, identified themselves with such terms as "Mexica,"
"Acolhua," and "Tenochca." It was through the immense
popularity of William H. Prescott's *The History of the
Conquest of Mexico* (1843) that the name "Aztec" came to
identify forever the various groups that made up the Mexica
kingdom. In this book I use the terms "Mexica" and "Aztec"
interchangeably because of the popularity of the latter
and the accuracy of the former. The two Mexica rulers
we call "Montezuma" were named Motecuhzoma
Ilhuicamina and Motecuhzoma Xocoyotzin respectively.
It was the latter who ruled between 1502 and 1520 and
entered the popular imagination of the English-speaking
world and the West as the king who ruled the "Halls of

Montezuma." I use the Nahuatl version to link these personages again to their real names.

Many thanks to three scholars who assisted me in the writing of this book: Eduardo Matos Moctezuma, Leonardo López Luján, and especially my collaborator of many years, Scott Sessions.

Chapter 1

The city of Tenochtitlan: center of the Aztec world

When Hernán Cortés led a Spanish army of five hundred soldiers, accompanied by several thousand skilled, allied native warriors, into the Aztec capital on November 8, 1519, the Europeans were filled with wonder by the enormous, splendid city in the middle of Lake Tezcoco. One of these soldiers, Bernal Díaz del Castillo, left this initial glimpse:

> [W]hen we saw so many cities and villages built in the water and other great towns on dry land and that straight and level Causeway going towards Mexico, we were amazed and said that it was like the enchantments they tell of in the legend of Amadís, on account of the great towers and pyramids rising from the water, and all built of masonry. And some of our soldiers even asked whether the things that we saw were not a dream…the appearance of the palaces in which they lodged us! How spacious and well built they were, of beautiful stone work and cedar wood, and the wood of other sweet scented trees, with great rooms and courts, wonderful to behold, covered with awnings of cotton cloth.

The size of the buildings and the great crowds who welcomed these strange-looking visitors left the Spaniards astonished. They saw huge palaces "coated with shiny cement and swept and garlanded…adjacent to great oratories for idols," some of which were covered with blood. The Aztec island capital, Tenochtitlan,

1

was at that time one of the largest cities in the world with nearly 200,000 inhabitants. Seville, the largest city known to most of the conquistadors, had 60,000 people, while London had closer to 50,000. The largest cities on earth, Paris and Constantinople, each had roughly 300,000 inhabitants.

Tenochtitlan, the "Great City of Mexico" as the Spaniards referred to it, was the supreme settlement of a political and economic empire made up of more than four hundred cities and towns spread through central Mesoamerica and extending into several distant southern and eastern areas. Tenochtitlan was the dominant sacred and political settlement of a Triple Alliance,

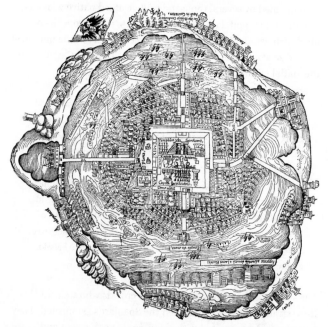

1. Engraved map of Tenochtitlan, embellished with several European pictorial conventions, from the first edition of Cortés's letters, printed in 1524.

which included the city-states of Tezcoco and Tlacopan. Together these three polities strove to control more than five million people spread over an area of more than 77,000 square miles. Yet this city's population, social complexity, and power was concentrated on an island of only 4.6 square miles, which actually combined the two separate settlements of Tlatelolco and Tenochtitlan into one core settlement. Radiating out from this island capital were more than a half-dozen causeways that linked it to nine smaller urban settlements on the nearby mainland and pushed the population of this megalopolis closer to 300,000 people. As the Spaniards quickly learned, the Aztec capital was both a garden city of great agricultural productivity and the center of a tributary empire that attracted and redistributed vast supplies of foodstuffs and commodities. This powerful economic system made Tenochtitlan the focus of Spanish envy and hopes for wealth and political domination. The centrality of the city and its linkage to a much wider ecological and political world became evident as the Spaniards toured the city. If we had been part of that tour in November and December of 1519, here is some of what we might have seen.

As the Spaniards walked along a major causeway toward the central ceremonial precinct, they saw the many bridges under which passed scores of canoes carrying people and goods to various neighborhoods and markets. They were soon greeted by "many more chieftains and caciques [who] approached clad in very rich mantles, the brilliant liveries of one chieftain different from those of another, and the causeways were crowded with them." Eventually the visitors saw the entourage of the ruler Motecuhzoma (He Who Grows Angry Like a Lord) Xocoyotzin (the Younger) approaching them. Known in Nahuatl as the *tlatoani*, or chief speaker, the king appeared "beneath a marvelously rich canopy of green-colored feathers with much gold and silver embroidery and with pearls and *chalchihuites* suspended from a sort of bordering, which was wonderful to look at." The "Great Montezuma" was adorned from head to foot as a living man-god who wore bejeweled sandals with soles of gold that never touched the earth, for other lords swept the ground and spread cloths before him. Surrounded by eight other richly dressed chieftains, four of whom supported a canopy over his head while the rest attended his every move and protected this man-god from intruders, the Aztec ruler greeted the Spaniards. Cortés, however, made an initial *faux pas*. He dismounted his horse and stepped forward with his arms outstretched to embrace the Aztec ruler. But as he neared Motecuhzoma's body several of the ruler's assistants strongly restrained him. The scene quickly recovered its sense of order through elaborate speeches of welcome by Motecuhzoma (aided by doña Marina—Cortés's Indian translator and mistress), which made it clear who was in charge and that the Spaniards were welcome guests. Soon the Spaniards were conducted to their quarters within the capital city. Motecuhzoma exchanged gifts with Cortés, giving him "a very rich necklace made of golden crabs, a marvelous piece of work, ... and three loads of mantles of rich feather work." Cortés reported in his letter to the king of Spain that he took off a necklace of pearls and cut glass that he was wearing and gave it to Motecuhzoma. Motecuhzoma spread his wealth around to Cortés's captains in the form of golden trinkets and feathered mantles, and gave each soldier a woven mantle.

In the following days the Spaniards visited "the great house full of ... books" (actually screenfold codices on which were painted the calendrical, historical, and geographical records of the empire) and then the royal armories "full of every sort of arms, many of them richly adorned with gold and precious stones, ... shields great and small, ... two-handed swords set with stone knives which cut much better than our swords." They then proceeded to an enormous aviary filled with countless species of birds "from the royal eagle ... and many other birds of great size, ... quetzals, ... from which they take the rich plumage which they use in their green featherwork." Spanish admiration turned to repulsion when they were led into the great "Idol House" containing not only "fierce gods" but many kinds of beasts of prey, including jaguars, wolves, and foxes, being fed with the flesh of other animals. Díaz del Castillo then added this ominous report: "I have heard it said that they feed them on the bodies of the Indians who have been sacrificed." Spanish admiration returned when their tour took them to lapidary and gold workshops where they saw jewelers working with precious stones and *chalchihuites*, which reminded the Spaniards of emeralds. They saw featherworkers, sculptors, weavers, and an immense quantity of fine fabrics with attractive and complex designs.

The Spaniards, always with an eye out for native women, were not disappointed when they saw large numbers of Motecuhzoma's beautifully dressed mistresses attending him and his nobles. They also viewed "nunneries" of young maidens being guarded and instructed by veteran "nuns." The Spaniards relaxed in lush gardens with sweet scented trees and medicinal herbs, and marveled at the luxurious homes of Aztec nobles.

Spanish interest in Aztec wealth escalated when the group arrived at the nearby imperial marketplace of Tlatelolco that, according to Cortés, was twice as large as the great market of Salamanca and filled with 60,000 people each day. Díaz del Castillo added that they "were astounded at the number of people and the quantity of merchandise that it contained, and at the good order and control that was maintained.... Each kind of merchandise was kept by itself and had its fixed place marked out." The weavers spinning many colors of cotton reminded some Spaniards of the silk market in Granada. What also greatly impressed the Spaniards were the various inspectors and magistrates who mediated disputes and kept order among the bustling crowds. At one point in their tour the Spaniards were taken to the top of one of the great pyramids for a bird's eye view of Tenochtitlan, which prompted Díaz del Castillo to make enthusiastic comparisons with the great cities of Europe: "we turned to look at the great marketplace and the crowds of people,...the murmur and hum of their voices and

5

words that they used could be heard more than a league off. Some of the soldiers among us who had been in many parts of the world, in Constantinople, and all over Italy, and in Rome, said that so large a marketplace and so full of people, and so well regulated and arranged, they had never beheld before."

Soon, the Spaniards witnessed a grand banquet presided over by Motecuhzoma, where more than thirty dishes, including rabbit, venison, wild boar, and many types of fowl, were prepared for him and his entourage of nobles, servants, and guards. The ruler sat on a soft and richly worked stool at a table with tablecloths of white cotton and was served by four beautiful women who brought him hand-washing bowls, towels, and tortilla bread. Seated behind a gold painted screen, he was joined by high government officials and family members with whom he shared the best dishes of the night, including fruit from distant regions of the empire as well as a chocolate drink made from cacao beans, which he drank in "cup-shaped vessels of pure gold." Entertainers showed up at some of these dinners: "some very ugly humpbacks...were their jesters, and other Indians, who must have been buffoons...told him witty sayings and others...sang and danced, for Motecuhzoma was fond of pleasure and song, and to these he ordered to be given what was left of the food and the jugs of cacao."

Then, Díaz del Castillo added a provocative and enigmatic passage about human sacrifice and cannibalism in relation to the feast: "I have heard it said that they were wont to cook for him the flesh of young boys, but as he had such a variety of dishes, made of so many things, we could not succeed in seeing if they were human flesh or of other things...so we had no insight into it."

The Spaniards saw many more places and cultural practices in the Aztec capital in the days and months following their initial tour. But within a year and a half of the Spanish arrival, the social order, architectural beauty, and neighborhoods of the entire island city were shattered and many thousands of people were killed by war and disease. The human price paid in this European and Mesoamerican encounter was tremendous on both sides but especially among the Aztecs, whose population would be decimated in the coming decades. While the Spaniards were, in the end, militarily and politically victorious, one of their chroniclers remembered their terrible defeat during the battle known as the Noche Triste: the Aztecs, fed up with Spanish abuses and the murders of a group of priests and dancers at a festival, attacked the intruders and drove them out of the city and into the waters. "The canal was soon choked with the bodies of men and horses. They filled the gap in the causeway with their own drowned bodies. Those who followed crossed to the other side by walking on the corpses." But the greatest laments were those of the Aztecs about their own destruction and defeat as is clear in this poet's words:

> We are crushed to the ground.
> We lie in ruins.
> There is nothing but grief and suffering in Mexico and Tlatelolco
> Where once we saw beauty and valor.

Díaz del Castillo shared this lament forty years later when he wrote: "Of all these things that I then beheld today all is overthrown and lost, nothing left standing."

Questions about the Aztecs

Once Europeans heard the astonishing reports of the discovery and conquest of Tenochtitlan and later read Spanish accounts of the indigenous riches, settlements, and religious practices "discovered" in New Spain, three major controversies developed. One question was whether Mesoamerican peoples had actually attained a level of social complexity and symbolic sophistication characteristic of urban civilization as reflected in the writings of Hernán Cortés and Bernal Díaz del Castillo. Were these accounts of cities and kings fanciful Spanish exaggerations designed to elevate the prestige of their military campaigns in the New World or were they generally accurate accounts of Aztec social life?

Another set of questions greatly challenged the Europeans: Where did these strangers, called "Indians," living in the new lands originally come from? Did they descend from Adam and Eve? Were they fully human and capable of understanding Christian teachings?

The third controversy, which continues to this day, was whether human sacrifice took place on the scale reported by the Spaniards and to what extent cannibalism was practiced. Did the Spaniards purposely exaggerate Aztec sacrifices to justify their military conquest of the city or to disguise the extent of their own violent practices? In this chapter we will address the first of these big questions while leaving the problem of human origins in the Americas and human sacrifice for later chapters.

The scientific rediscovery of the Aztec world

Almost immediately following the collapse of Tenochtitlan, an aggressive conversion effort was launched to wipe out Aztec religion and replace it with a brand of Roman Catholicism that would herald in the millennium prophesied at the end of the New Testament. A clear example of this impassioned campaign to overwhelm and transform the misguided and dangerous life ways of the Aztecs is seen in this passage from the Franciscan friar Martín de Valencia's *obediencia* (exhortation and instructions) given to the "apostolic twelve" missionaries who were sent to Mexico City in 1524 to officially begin the evangelization of the natives. Using a series of martial metaphors, which defined their purposes as a kind of holy war, their *superior* implored them to attack and utterly defeat the evil madness of Aztec thought and culture: "Go ... armed with the shield of faith and with the breastplate of justice, with the blade of the spirit of salvation, with the helmet and lance of perseverance... and to the perfidious infidels a road may be opened for them and pointed out, and the madness of heretical evil may fall apart and come to nothing." In fact, when those twelve Franciscans arrived in Mexico, Cortés arranged a ceremonial escort from Veracruz all the way to the destroyed capital of Tenochtitlan so that their arrival and purpose could be witnessed everywhere they triumphantly walked.

But the process of converting the "perfidious infidels" ran into problems when European priests and laypeople began to interact with native peoples who spoke the indigenous languages, knew native philosophical teachings, and could communicate the myths, songs, histories, and cultural practices of pre-Hispanic times. A significant number of texts began to emerge that described indigenous cultural practices, settlements, calendars, and mythologies of many city-states and rural communities. A Franciscan friar, Bernardino de Sahagún, produced a twelve-book chronicle of the Aztec world known today as the *Florentine Codex*. His interviews with elders between the 1530s and 1570s reveal a sophisticated social, linguistic, and ceremonial world in which merchants and kings, slaves and warriors, women and men, farmers and shamans, and priests and artists interacted to produce a highly stratified, intensely ritualized, wealthy urban society. But even as Sahagún, his students, and other friars collected and recorded this kind of knowledge, there were intense cultural and religious forces in colonial society working against their dissemination. Without necessarily intending to do so, Sahagún had produced a huge amount of writing that some Spaniards believed was *preserving* Aztec knowledge, mythology, and cultural practices.

In the sixteenth and seventeenth centuries, as missionaries and civil servants collected data on Aztec life, the majority of the native inhabitants suffered terrible diseases and were forced to provide cheap labor while being confronted with unrelenting evangelical efforts. These pressures on indigenous peoples greatly

9

weakened their physical and psychological well-being and impeded serious or reasonable evaluations of the nature and extent of these new social realities. As the archaeologist Eduardo Matos Moctezuma, excavator of the Great Aztec Temple, said about late sixteenth-century Mexico, "The Aztec world appeared to be a dead civilization, while the society of New Spain came to vigorous life. The initial interest in the pre-Hispanic past gave way to a confidence that it was buried forever."

It was not until the end of the eighteenth century that a revival of interest in understanding the nature of Aztec society took place. As independence movements against Spain grew in Mexico and other Latin American countries, people developed a concomitant interest in looking backwards to the achievements of native civilization in the Americas. The Creoles (Spaniards born and bred in New Spain) of the colonies, as well as some educated Mestizos (individuals of mixed Spanish and indigenous ancestry) who were now feeling the need to distinguish their identities and political life from imperial Spain, began to use evidence of Aztec and other indigenous civilizations as symbols of opposition to being ruled by Spaniards across the ocean. It was in this politically charged atmosphere that the first major discoveries of Aztec sculptures took place in 1790 in the heart of Mexico City and led to a new public awareness of the great cultural achievements of pre-Hispanic Mesoamerica.

The process of resurfacing the Zócalo (main square) that year by order of Viceroy Juan Vicente de Güemes Padilla Horcasitas yielded the sensational discoveries of two giant monoliths: one depicting the earth goddess Coatlicue (Serpent Skirt) and the other, the circular Sun Stone (also known as the Calendar Stone). Both of these monuments were magnificently carved, and the Sun Stone, in particular, with its complex design and intricate glyphic language, reflected a highly sophisticated culture. These treasures stimulated an intense interest in the Aztec world after centuries of neglect.

In 1792 the Mexican astronomer and anthropologist Antonio de León y Gama published a widely read essay about the discovery of the monuments, emphasizing the "great knowledge possessed by the Indians of this America in the arts and sciences in the time of their paganism." The people who made these stones were not "irrational or simpleminded" but rather represented an "excellence" of culture in human history, "for without knowing iron or steel, they sculptured with great perfection from hard stone the statues that represent their false idols; and they made other architectural works, using for their labors other more solid and hard stones instead of tempered chisels and steel picks." The Creole leaders in Mexico faced the challenge of where to put these monumental sculptures of Aztec genius and paganism. Should they make them public and stir up a full-fledged public fascination with the Aztecs or hide them from plain sight? León y Gama had encouraged officials to transport the many-ton Coatlicue to the Royal and Pontifical University so as to place it "in the most conspicuous spot in that building, taking care,...to have it measured, weighed, drawn, and engraved so that it may be published." But when the great German explorer and scientist Alexander von Humboldt arrived in Mexico City in 1802 and asked to study the huge Aztec stone sculpture, he was told that the Coatlicue had been buried underneath one of the corridors of the university. Those officials still loyal to Spain's distant rule had decided to keep the colossal image of the Aztec earth goddess out of sight because it could become a powerful symbol that New Spain had a distinct identity from the motherland. Through the influence of a bishop who persuaded the university rector to unearth the statue, Humboldt was able to study the Aztec sculpture firsthand.

The association of Aztec culture with high civilization found another champion in Servando Teresa de Mier, who delivered an ironic sermon on December 12, 1794, the annual feast day of the Mexican Virgin of Guadalupe. The friar identified what he considered the best parts of Aztec society with the ancient presence in Mexico of one of Jesus's disciples. In a harsh criticism of colonial officials who he thought were politically corrupt, he claimed that the glory of the conquest of Mexico was not due to the Spaniards but had been initiated more than a thousand years earlier when Saint Thomas appeared in the New World—now remembered in the indigenous stories of the man-god Quetzalcoatl (Plumed Serpent) who had governed the ancient Toltec kingdom when prosperity and peace ruled the land. Mier claimed that the Toltec holy man who was revered by native peoples for inventing astronomy, building a great capital, and creating a dignified religious philosophy was not an indigenous hero at all. This meant that the Aztecs had indeed created a real civilization *but* that its greatest parts reflected an ancient Christianity that had enriched Mesoamerica long before the Europeans arrived. He further argued that the image of the Virgin of Guadalupe had been actually painted on Saint Thomas's cloak in the first century, and not in the sixteenth century on the Indian Juan Diego's cloak, as the faithful in Mexico had come to believe. Again, the Spanish Crown was the target of this eighteenth-century "culture war."

The most elaborate example of the debate about Aztec social complexity was expressed in the nineteenth-century work of Lewis H. Morgan, one of the founders of the academic discipline of anthropology in the United States and author of an influential book titled *Ancient Society*. Morgan had developed a three-stage typology of human progress: savagery, barbarism, and civilization. He insisted the Aztecs had developed only to the stage of barbarism and could not be compared to civilized societies. Morgan was upset that so many major writers and scholars since the sixteenth century had naively believed that Díaz del Castillo and other "eyewitnesses" had accurately described the Aztec society as a developed urban civilization. One of Morgan's main targets was the highly influential work of William H. Prescott whose runaway 1843 best seller *History of the Conquest of Mexico* (with ten editions published in England and twenty-three in the United

States) celebrated the Aztecs as people of extraordinary social and cultural accomplishments. Prescott's work on Mexico was considered by his admirers as the greatest achievement in American historical writing up to that time.

Intellectually scandalized by the historian's claims, influence, and fame, Morgan vehemently argued that Prescott had penned "a cunningly wrought fable" and started the construction of an "Aztec Romance" wherein they and their predecessors had achieved a level of social complexity akin to real civilizations of the "Old World," something that most nineteenth-century anthropologists considered impossible. According to Morgan, the idea that an American Indian tribe had risen to the level of "civilization" threatened the development of serious scientific progress in the social sciences. In his essay "Montezuma's Dinner," Morgan asserted that the Aztecs were still a "breech cloth people wearing the rag of barbarism as an unmistakable evidence of their condition." Spanish accounts of native American civilization were really the "gossip of a camp of soldiers suddenly cast into an earlier form of society, which the village of Indians, of America, of all mankind, best represented.... Upon this rhapsody [of descriptions of palaces] it will be sufficient to remark that halls were entirely unknown in Indian architecture." Morgan, who claimed to see the Aztec city more clearly 350 years after the Spaniards, concluded that "there was neither a political society, nor a state, nor any civilization in America when it was discovered, and, excluding the Eskimos, but one race of Indians, the Red Race."

This irrational and entrenched view of the nature of Aztec social complexity began to change seriously with innovative scholarship in Mexico in the early decades of the twentieth century. The father of modern Mexican anthropology, Manuel Gamio, developed new research models that emphasized multidisciplinary studies in the investigations of pre-Aztec cities. From 1911 to 1925 he investigated a series of key archaeological sites in Mexico and uncovered evidence of very early urban settlements in and around the Basin of Mexico including Cuicuilco (700–150 BCE) and Teotihuacan (1–550 CE). Gamio combined the study of myth, historical sources, archaeological remains, and geographic settings with sculpture, human remains, flora and fauna, and especially ceramic evidence to achieve a new historical understanding of pre-Hispanic development in Mesoamerica that effectively demolished the views of Morgan.

A brilliant advance in knowledge about pre-Aztec urban life in Mesoamerica took place in 1931 when the innovative Mexican archaeologist Alfonso Caso discovered and excavated an elite tomb at the mountaintop ceremonial city of Monte Albán (500 BCE–800 CE) in Oaxaca. Following the discovery of extremely fine ritual objects in Tomb 7 at Monte Albán, Caso and his colleague Ignacio Bernal excavated in the Great Plaza and uncovered 180 tombs, palaces, and monuments with inscriptions and complex iconography. This led to Caso's worldwide fame and an emerging view of the origin of urban life in pre-Hispanic Mexico going back, in the case of Monte Albán, to between 500 and 100 BCE.

Then, in 1943, the German-Mexican scholar Paul Kirchhoff combined accounts like Díaz del Castillo's with linguistic, cultural, and archaeological evidence to define, for the first time in full scholarly fashion, a complex, sophisticated, socially stratified cultural area he called Mesoamerica. In a groundbreaking essay he identified Mesoamerica geographically as the southern two-thirds of Mexico plus Guatemala, Belize, El Salvador, and parts of Honduras, Nicaragua, and Costa Rica. In this area socially stratified patterns of settlement, bureaucratic structures, long- and short-distance trading networks, linguistic practices, and cultural systems evolved over two millennia prior to the arrival of the Spaniards. Mesoamerica was an urban-oriented world well before the rise of the Aztec empire in the fifteenth century.

This developing picture of pre-Aztec and Aztec urbanism has been filled out in the second half of the twentieth century by archaeological projects and the decipherment of codices and inscriptions. Continuing work at sites such as Teotihuacan, Tula, Monte Albán, El Tajín, and in the Maya area clearly demonstrates that Mesoamerica indeed is one of the seven areas of primary urban generation on earth. The most spectacular and significant scientific advance in our understanding of the Aztecs, however, has been taking place since 1978 in downtown Mexico City where the excavation of the Great Aztec Temple, the very structure that Díaz del Castillo described, is discovering the foundations, sculptures, human and animal burials, jewelry, musical instruments, and god images of Tenochtitlan's central shrine. Directed by Eduardo Matos Moctezuma, this high-powered archaeological project has uncovered seven major rebuildings of the Great Temple and more than 125 rich caches that the Aztec priests buried in the floors as ritual offerings to their war god Huitzilopochtli, the rain god Tlaloc, and other deities.

Utilizing these spectacular discoveries, scholars have shown that in fifteenth- and early sixteenth-century Mexico, the city of Tenochtitlan was the supreme place of political and religious power upon which a vision of empire was founded. This capital, and especially its monumental ceremonial center, imperial marketplace, and abundant agricultural gardens, so enthusiastically described by Díaz del Castillo, was the place where Aztec culture, authority, and domination were expressed in buildings, stone, sound, myth, public spectacles, and sacrifices. Tenochtitlan was a gathering place of pilgrims, traders, ambassadors, diplomats, nobles, farmers, craftspeople, and even the numerous enemy warriors who were brought to the capital for sacrificial ceremonies. An aged Aztec priest who described the powers of Tenochtitlan and Motecuhzoma over the many cities and towns that were conquered by the Aztecs remembered that the conquered people "brought their tribute; their goods,...the green stone, the gold, the precious feathers,...the fine turquoise, the lovely continga, the roseate spoonbill. They gave it to Motecuhzoma."

Chapter 2
Aztec foundations: Aztlan, cities, peoples

It often takes a poet to find the right words to capture such an extraordinary place and story as Mexico City. The Mexican novelist Carlos Fuentes said it best when he described the capital as a "city of fixed sun,…city ancient in light,…witness to all we forget,…old city cradled among birds of omen,…city in the true image of gigantic heaven. Incandescent prickly pear."

The "bird" and "prickly pear" allusions in this passage relate to the central emblem of the Mexican flag where an eagle devours a serpent upon a blooming cactus, which grows out of a stylized rock in the blue waters of Lake Tezcoco. This dramatic image refers to the crucial moment in the Aztec foundation myths when their Chichimec ancestors arrived in the Basin of Mexico at the beginning of the fourteenth century after a long and arduous journey from their distant homeland in the north. According to one tradition, it was at this exact spot where the eagle landed that the Aztecs built the first shrine to their patron god Huitzilopochtli (Southern Hummingbird), who had led them southward on their journey. This image of a triumphant, god-sanctioned arrival in the Basin of Mexico was central to the Aztec claim of being inheritors of a civilizing urban tradition, which reached back hundreds of years to the sacred capitals of Teotihuacan, Tula, and Cholula. Each was constructed on earth to be in "the true image of gigantic heaven" and served as models in an Aztec sacred history depicted in architecture, picture writing, and song.

Out of Aztlan: sacred history

Tenochtitlan appeared in Bernal Díaz del Castillo's tour as a grand unity of architecture, order, and brilliance. But the story of its rise from the muddy lakebeds in the Basin of Mexico is one of unrelenting struggle, rivalries, conflict, suffering, and eventual triumph. The founders of the city are referred to variously as "Azteca," "Mexica," or "Tenochca" in the most reliable sources, indicating that a number of different ethnic groups migrated into the basin, eventually coming together to form the "Triple Alliance" of Tezcoco, Tenochtitlan-Tlatelolco, and Tlacopan. In spite of the diversity of documents and different versions of Aztec sacred history (a mixture of myths and historical memories), we are able to identify basic patterns of an epic odyssey, which included the emergence from an ancient homeland, followed by a pilgrimage that lasted many years under the inspiration of a patron deity and warrior-priests. This long journey stopped at specific places memorialized in Aztec history with miraculous events, which led to their ultimate arrival at the place where the eagle appeared on the blooming nopal. After a period of poverty and servitude, the Aztecs struggled, farmed, fought, and negotiated themselves into a position of regional dominance. The social symbol of their successes was the architectural and economic nexus known as Tenochtitlan, rooted in civilized traditions going back more than a thousand years to ancient Teotihuacan (1–550 CE) and Tula (900–1100 CE) and their contemporary neighbors at Cholula (100–1521 CE), located on the other side of the volcanoes Popocatepetl and Iztaccihuatl.

According to ethnohistorical sources, the ancestors emerged from a fertile hill known as Chicomoztoc (Place of Seven Caves) and inhabited Aztlan (Place of White Heron), an ancient settlement surrounded by water, whose people accordingly were called

"Azteca." Their emergence and journey were prompted by a shaman's dream or a message from their patron deity Huitzilopochtli, who ordered them to depart and seek a new homeland. In the *Codex Aubin*, Huitzilopochtli gave the Azteca a new name upon their departure from Aztlan—"Mexica," from which came the name "Mexicans"—and three gifts that forever marked their cultural practices: the arrow, the bow, and the net.

2. Aztec ancestors emerge from Chicomoztoc, the "Place of Seven Caves."

With their new identity as Mexica, now able to hunt and fight with their weapons and catch birds and fish with their nets, they began their sacred quest. In the next two centuries this transformation into Mexica became part of the model for their lives as aggressive militarists, skillful fishermen, and productive farmers. They traveled in groups called *calpolli*, which, once they settled in the Basin of Mexico, became the basis for their military units and tribute redistribution. Each *calpolli* consisted of a group of families united by a common deified ancestor.

Their long journey was marked by other exemplary changes, none more so than when their odyssey came to the sacred hill of Coatepetl (Serpent Mountain). Arriving at this auspicious location, still far from their final home, the Mexica built a settlement oriented toward the four directions of the universe— East, North, West, and South—and constructed a dam in a nearby lake. The result was a fertile lagoon that encouraged the rapid growth of flowers, plants, and animals that provided food, beauty, and crucial elements for their ritual life. This new settlement was both an elaborate copy of the Aztlan they had left and a model for the city of Tenochtitlan they would build in Lake Tezcoco. While they began to thrive in this location, their patron god Huitzilopochtli and his main devotees insisted that this was not the endpoint of their journey and that they had to move on toward their future homeland. This occasioned a harsh conflict between Huitzilopochtli's followers and those led by a woman warrior named Coyolxauhqui (Painted Bells), who refused to rejoin the pilgrimage to a distant shore. Hostilities erupted and the loyal followers of Huitzilopochtli attacked at midnight, killed the rebels, and sacrificed their leader Coyolxauhqui. From this moment Huitzilopochtli's cult became dominant among the victorious group of Mexica who pressed on in their journey.

This episode, as recounted in various primary texts and sculpture, refers to actual historical events where two political factions fought for dominance. In time, this social conflict was transformed into a sacred, official history stating that Coatepec was the mythic site of a cosmic battle between the sun and the moon in which the solar deity triumphed. This combination of "hill-lagoon-battle" at Coatepec was transformed, in popular memory, into the rituals and religious architecture of the Great Aztec Temple that stood at the center of Tenochtitlan. The Aztecs built their entire capital around a temple-pyramid symbolizing this Serpent Mountain and carried out various human sacrifices of enemy warriors who were identified with the losing cult of Coyolxauhqui (the moon goddess) during the pilgrimage from Aztlan.

A series of sources such as the *Mapa Sigüenza, Codex Xolotl, Mapa Quinatzin, Codex Aubin*, and the recently rediscovered *Mapa de Cuauhtinchan No. 2* (depicting a different group's pilgrimage along an alternative route but with striking similarities) shows migrants leaving Chicomoztoc, traveling along difficult pathways, scouting lands from nearby hills, performing rituals, confronting other peoples, conferring with patron deities, and settling for periods of time at such places as Tenayuca, Huexotla, and Tezcoco. Along the way marriage alliances were made, territories organized in different sized units, and fishing and farming areas set up as the Mexica and other migrant groups gradually became integrated into the more ancient urban society in and around the Basin of Mexico. The religious vision animating these efforts is evident in this command given by their patron god Huitzilopochtli through his shaman priests. Clearly reflecting a post-journey perspective, the god made an imperial-sized promise: "We shall proceed to establish ourselves and settle down, and we shall conquer all peoples of the universe; and I tell you in all truth that I will make you lords and kings of all that is in the world; and when you become rulers, you shall have countless and infinite numbers of vassals, who will pay tribute to you."

In truth, the Mexica journey into the Basin of Mexico was fraught with resistance in spite of Huitzilopochtli's reassurance of a smooth rise to dominance. The sacred histories tell us that the

Mexica visited the great ceremonial capital of Tula, then went down the coast of Lake Tezcoco where they visited Tenayuca and arrived at Chapultepec (Grasshopper Hill), highly valued for its freshwater springs. Settling at Chapultepec, they passed a period of twenty-five years of struggle, conflict, and eventual victory. The key episode took place when Copil, a distant relative and rival of their leader Huitzilopochtli, attacked the Mexica community in order to cast them out from the lakeshore. In the battle that followed, Copil was captured and sacrificed, and in an act of triumph and insult a Mexica priest tossed his heart across the water to land on a marshy island.

The narrative tells of a most ignominious ritual carried out by the Mexica, who were then forced out to an obscure island in the middle of Lake Tezcoco. According to one text, the Mexica orchestrated the marriage of one of their leaders to the daughter of one of the lords of Colhuacan, the ruling dynasty in the area. The Mexica promised the ruler that his daughter would be greatly honored as the "wife of Huitzilopochtli." Not realizing the true and terrible fate that awaited her, the Colhua lord sent his daughter to Tizaapan for the wedding. In a ritual marriage to the patron deity, the daughter was splendidly arrayed and then sacrificed at the local temple. Her body was flayed in a ceremony symbolizing the renewal of plants, which don new skins each spring. When Achitometl saw his daughter's skin draped over a dancing Mexica priest, he was outraged and ordered his troops to attack the Mexica and drive them in a rain of darts out into uninhabited land in the middle of the lake.

To what extent this episode is a combination of legend and history cannot be known. Suffice it to say that the previous pattern of separation from a valued location, a journey to an unknown land, and a change in social status was repeated again as the Mexica began to transform their marshy, no-man's-land island into, at first, a modest ceremonial settlement and eventually into the great urban center of Tenochtitlan.

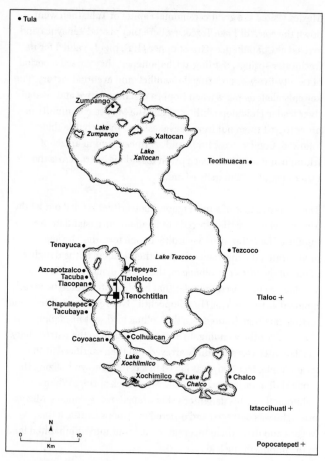

3. Map of the Basin of Mexico, ca. 1519.

The Mexica later claimed that when they first arrived, beaten and yet defiant on the island, one of their priests had a vision of the earlier triumph of Huitzilopochtli in which he saw where Copil's heart had been thrown years before. The Mexica turned to that location and saw the giant eagle perched on the blooming prickly pear cactus, marking the exact spot where they would build their first temple to Huitzilopochtli. One account reads that they saw Huitzilopochtli in the form of an eagle, "with his wings stretched outward like the rays of the sun." They humbled themselves, and the god "humbled himself, bowing his head low in their direction."

Another version says that one of the priests who saw the eagle dived into the lake and disappeared. When the priest failed to surface, his companions thought that he had drowned, and they retired to their camp. Later, the priest returned and announced that he had descended into the underworld, where he met the rain god Tlaloc and was given permission for the Mexica to settle in this sacred place. Thus they had both the forces of the sky (the eagle, Huitzilopochtli) and of the earth (the lake god, Tlaloc) granting permission to build the new center of the world. The great journey from Chicomoztoc and Aztlan was now complete, and at a site uncannily like the fertile island community from which they originally set out, the Mexica got down to the work of building Tenochtitlan.

Early on, the Aztec settlement was divided into four segments around a ceremonial center consisting of a main temple dedicated to Huitzilopochtli and other religious buildings. Duality was a fundamental cosmological idea among the Mexica, and their many *calpolli* were united within a dual governmental structure. One part of the government was run by a *teachcauh* or "elder brother" chosen by the *calpolli* to be in charge of internal affairs such as land management, temples and schools, the defense of the community, and the modest tribute payments they garnered. The other part of the government was run by the *tecuhtli*, named by the king (*tlatoani*) to act as judge, military commander, tax collector, and mediator between the ruler's court and the various *calpolli*. In effect, each *calpolli* located in one of the four quarters of the settlement acted as a military unit in the overall army and paid tribute to the ruler's family and palace.

During the early stages of settlement a major land conflict erupted, and some *calpolli* broke off from the community on the island of Tenochtitlan. They moved to a nearby island-lagoon they named Tlatelolco, which grew into a powerful rival due to its large marketplace that was later fully integrated into Tenochtitlan's sphere of influence.

Even with this developing cohesion and organization, the Mexica of Tenochtitlan had limited cultural and political legitimacy in the eyes of more established communities. They desperately needed to gain access to the prestige and power associated with the revered Toltec cultural traditions located in the city-state of Colhuacan. The Aztecs were able to make this crucial alliance when the ruler of Colhuacan accepted their proposal to place a prince named Acamapichtli, a Colhuacan noble who also had Mexica blood, on the Tenochtitlan throne. The Aztecs had now made the step up the social ladder by gaining this political access to the ruling families who traced their lineages back to the Toltecs (900–1100 CE) of the great priest-king Topiltzin Quetzalcoatl. But it also meant they were clearly under the domination of Colhuacan whose capital was Azcapotzalco, the leading Toltec-descended military power of the region.

Splendid cities before the Aztecs

In the centuries prior to the Mexica migrations into the Basin of Mexico, there were several great urban settlements, which became the centers of political power and sacred authority in central Mesoamerica. The most outstanding were Teotihuacan, Tula, and Cholula. Each had profound influences on the history and identity of Tenochtitlan. This urban lineage became evident when Mexican archaeologists dug into the layers of the foundations of the Great Aztec Temple (1390s–1521 CE), beginning in 1978. They discovered sculptures, masks, and architectural styles representing a more ancient cultural fabric of diverse peoples, urban places, and complex religious traditions going back a thousand years before the rise of Tenochtitlan.

Even though the earliest shrine found at the Great Aztec Temple dates from the mid-fourteenth century, archaeologists found abundant evidence that the Aztecs had a deep cultural memory carried by priests, rulers, and artists who claimed descent and legitimacy from Toltec Tula (900–1100 CE) and Teotihuacan (1–550 CE). For example, two "Red Temples," excavated on the south and north sides of the main pyramid, have architectural styles and murals that represent the symbolism of ancient Teotihuacan. And several prominent sculptures at the Great Aztec Temple are direct imitations of sculptures made in Tula, seventy miles to the north of Tenochtitlan, and associated with Quetzalcoatl, the Feathered Serpent ruler-god remembered as the originator of the calendar, ritual practices, and wisdom. These sculptures found in the heart of the Aztec city reflect Toltec era art styles that had spread far and wide to various regional capitals in Mesoamerica. The depth of this historical concern is reflected in one tantalizing discovery in a burial cache at the Great Aztec Temple of a mint-condition Olmec mask dated from around 1000 BCE. But most of all, the Aztecs turned to Teotihuacan, City of the Gods, for inspiration, political authority, and mythic legitimacy.

Teotihuacan: city of the gods

If there was one ancient city that attracted the attention of its contemporaries *and* its successors in Mesoamerica it was the massive capital of Teotihuacan (1–550 CE). It certainly attracted the attention of the Aztec ruling house and especially the two Motecuhzomas, Motecuhzoma Ilhuicamina (1440–63) and his nephew Motecuhzoma Xocoyotzin (1502–20). The first

Motecuhzoma, who managed a substantial expansion of Aztec landholdings and military domination, commissioned the building of a large ritual platform along the Street of the Dead in Teotihuacan, in front of the gigantic Pyramid of the Sun. Even though the ancient city, located to the northeast of Tenochtitlan, was already largely in ruins by Motecuhzoma I's time, the place was viewed as the true cultural and political hearth of subsequent city-states and peoples. The Aztecs did some archaeology of their own, digging up prized caches of objects (including ritual masks) and then burying them at their Great Temple. The second Motecuhzoma, believing that the city had been built and populated by giants, made periodic visits to the site to pay homage and draw religious legitimacy from the sacred ancestors residing there. In Mexica creation mythology, Teotihuacan was the place of the spectacular creation of the Fifth Sun, the cosmic era in which the Aztecs resided.

What impressed the Aztecs when they visited the site, even when it was largely abandoned, was its monumentality and its superb urban design, murals, architecture, and artwork, showing that these ancients had a ritual life dedicated to agriculture, warfare, ballgames, deities, dynasties, and sacrificial burials. When Bernardino de Sahagún interviewed Aztec elders in Tenochtitlan during the 1550s, they recited for him the great creation myth linking their own city and era to the dawn of time in Teotihuacan. Reading the myth today, we know that the Aztecs were talking as much about how they saw themselves as how they saw their ancestors carrying out sky-watching, prayer, ceremonies, and ritual sacrifices to their many gods.

The younger native scribes, listening to their elders talking to Sahagún, recorded a story that began in the mythic past, fifty-two years after the previous cosmic age had collapsed into darkness: "It is told that when all was in darkness, when yet no sun had shown and no dawn had broken, ... the gods gathered themselves there at Teotihuacan. They spoke ... 'Who will take it upon himself to be the sun, to bring the dawn?'" The story tells of two volunteers who stepped forward before the sacred hearth where a fire had been burning. Two gods, Nanahuatzin (Pimply One) and Tecuciztecatl (Lord of Snails) prepared themselves for ritual self-immolation. The virile Lord of Snails approached the fire several times but became frightened by the intense heat. The Pimply One then came forward with courageous resolve and cast himself into the fire, his body crackling and sizzling. The other god followed, and the two emerged from the fire in the forms of powerful animals—an eagle and a jaguar—that later became the patrons of the two main Aztec warrior groups.

Then, in a gesture that was crucial to the Aztecs when thinking about the great ancestors of Teotihuacan, other gods sacrificed themselves in the fire and under the sacrificial knife to give life and energy to the sun. The sun was born on the eastern horizon and, after wobbling in the sky for a period of time prior to more sacrifices, it ascended the sky and began its long pattern of passages through the heavens and the underworld. The Aztecs came to believe that this cosmic event of *incremental sacrifice*— the ritual increase from sacrificing one individual to sacrificing many individuals followed by the rising of the sun—brought the cosmos they now inhabited into being.

Known today as "The Pyramids," Teotihuacan is the most visited archaeological site in the Americas. Visitors can see not only that it contained monumental architecture, including the so-called Pyramids of the Sun and of the Moon and the great Street of the Dead, but they learn that the entire city was designed as an image of the cosmos. In a special way, Teotihuacan's beginnings parallel a key symbol in the later Aztec story of origins in Chicomoztoc, for Teotihuacan had its beginnings in a cave. Excavations carried out in the 1970s showed that directly beneath the largest building in the site, the Pyramid of the Sun (the third largest pyramid in the world, next to the giant structure at Cholula and the Great Pyramid of Giza) lie the remains of an ancient tunnel, cave, and

27

shrine area that served as one of the earliest centers for rituals and offerings to the gods of the underworld.

Throughout Mesoamerican history, caves were valued as the place of origin of ancestral peoples who were identified with the life giving forces found in seeds, water, and terrestrial beings. Caves were also "passageways" to the underworld, and rituals performed in caves could symbolically transport human beings into the realms of the world below. The cave beneath the Pyramid of the Sun was decorated and artificially reshaped to form a four-petalled flower. The Teotihuacan Mapping Project, a massive research program carried out in the 1970s, revealed that the entire inhabited space of the city was laid out by its planners and architects as a four-part metropolis, which conformed in various ways to the structure of the cosmos. The city's hundreds of residential, ritual, and commercial buildings were organized into an intricate grid pattern emanating from the north–south "Street of the Dead" (named by archaeologists) and the east–west avenue, which crossed at right angles in the center of the city.

By around 450 CE, Teotihuacan had become the dominant city-state of central Mesoamerica, populated by more than 150,000 people. Ongoing archaeological work at the site reveals that the prestige of this capital's buildings, mural art, ritual spectacles, and political power influenced many cities and towns within and beyond the central plateau of Mexico, including the mighty Zapotecs in Oaxaca and the Maya kings of distant Copán in northern Honduras. Since 2000, new evidence has shown that Teotihuacan's power to influence major political decisions and alliances extended to the rituals and architecture of the royal house of Copán. Its influence also extended through time, reaching into the minds of the Aztecs and other communities of the sixteenth century.

Although many parts of Teotihuacan were excavated in the twentieth century, it has only been since the 1980s that archaeologists have discovered significant ritual burials *inside* its major ceremonial structures. In the Pyramid of Quetzalcoatl archaeologists found a host of sacrificial victims with their hands bound behind their backs, wearing necklaces of human mandibles. Alongside these individuals were objects pointing to the ritual cults of fertility and warfare that remained the fundamental foci of religious and political life up to and throughout the Aztec empire. Work at the Pyramid of the Moon uncovered similar sacrificial remains, along with precious jades from the Maya area. At the present time, new excavations underway inside the gigantic Pyramid of the Sun should tell us more about the prestige, ritual life, and extensive reach of this "Abode of the Gods" whose style of life both haunted and inspired the Aztecs when they were building their own ceremonial precinct seven hundred years later.

Tollan: city of the Feathered Serpent

When Bernardino de Sahagún and other investigators queried the Aztec elders about their history, they were repeatedly told about a magnificent kingdom called Tollan or Tula where the great Toltecs had been ruled, before being abandoned, by a priest-king named Topiltzin Quetzalcoatl (Our Young Prince, the Plumed Serpent). In fact, from the twelfth century on in Mesoamerica, a rich tradition of stories, songs, paintings, and sculptures concerning the inspiring career and achievements of Quetzalcoatl survives. Sahagún's informants recalled that "Truly with him it began, truly from him it flowed out, from Quetzalcoatl, all art and knowledge." In Aztec times, their high priests were given the title of "Quetzalcoatl," and they taught their children the story of his kingdom as well as his loss of power and disappearance into the eastern sea and his prophesied return.

The sacred history of the Toltecs and Quetzalcoatl celebrated the brilliance and stability of a great city-state, which one text calls the "Great Tollan." The Aztecs claimed that the "Tolteca were wise.

Their works were all good, all perfect, all wonderful, all miraculous; their houses beautiful, tiled in mosaics, smoothed, stuccoed, very marvelous." This passage sounds remarkably similar to Bernal Díaz del Castillo's dreamy descriptions of Tenochtitlan and points to the prestige the Toltec capital held in Aztec memory. Reflecting their own sense of purpose, the Aztec stories about the Toltecs celebrated the unparalleled agricultural abundance and cultural achievements that linked gods and humans closely together. All "the squashes were very large, and some quite round. And the ears of maize were as large as hand grinding stones, and long. They could hardly be embraced in one's arms." The cotton fields glowed in many colors including "chili-red, yellow, pink, brown, green, blue, verdigris color, dark brown, ripening brown, dark blue, fine yellow, coyote-colored.... All of these came exactly so; they did not dye them." This paradise on earth was peopled by the finest artists, featherworkers, architects, and astronomers who were revered for having invented the calendar and who aligned the city with the cardinal directions of the universe. And in the center of all this abundance, cultural creativity, and skill stood Quetzalcoatl, the great Aztec ancestor, who was "looked upon as a god. He was worshiped and prayed to in former times in Tollan, and there his temple stood; very high, very tall. Extremely tall, extremely high."

The site that archaeologists identify with the Toltec kingdom, however, appears much more modest in size and splendor than what the Aztec elders eulogized to Sahagún. Spread out over several hilltops in the present-day Mexican state of Hidalgo, Tula, while impressive with its ceremonial center of palaces, pyramids, ballcourts, carved friezes, and monumental sculpture, is dwarfed by the city of Teotihuacan, which collapsed several centuries before the rise of Toltec Tula. Could it be that the Aztecs were recalling traditions of urban greatness reaching back through the Toltec kingdom of the tenth to the twelfth centuries and grasping the urban image of magnificent Teotihuacan but calling it Tollan?

Cholula: the pilgrimage capital

Cholula, the third city of these great Mesoamerican precursor capitals, was still socially active and politically influential in Aztec times, unlike Teotihuacan and Tula-Tollan. This pilgrimage capital still contains the largest pyramid in the world and is located on a plain just east of two of Mesoamerica's most significant volcanoes, Iztaccihuatl (White Woman) and Popocatepetl (Smoking Mountain). When Cortés and the Spaniards made their decision in 1519 to march across the mountains and valleys to Motecuhzoma's Tenochtitlan, they learned from their Tlaxcalan allies that Cholula stood in their way. Cholula was one of the oldest inhabited cities in the Americas, and its illustrious history was partly due to its strategic location in the center of the Puebla-Tlaxcala region, which opened transportation pathways to more southern and eastern sections of Mesoamerica. Both Cortés and Díaz del Castillo marveled at the number of religious buildings it had. Cortés wrote that "it is the city most suited for Spaniards to live in that I have seen" in Mexico, and they compared it to Valladolid, Spain. What impressed the European invaders were the thousands of pilgrims visiting Cholula's shrines, temples, and marketplace. It reminded them of Rome and Mecca, the sacred pilgrimage centers par excellence of Christianity and Islam.

As with almost all regional capitals in Mesoamerica, Cholula was a compact ceremonial center with pyramids, temples, palaces, grand staircases, an acropolis, stelae, and murals. The supreme role played by its Great Pyramid, Tlachihualtepetl (Man-Made Mountain) is often mentioned in the surviving literature and is also evident in the archaeology. Well before the Spaniards entered the city, the Great Pyramid had been expanded to 1,165 feet wide—larger than any of the great pyramids of Egypt. Constructed over the course of a 1,700-year period, its cosmic significance includes the fact that, like the Pyramid of the Sun in Teotihuacan, it was situated above a natural spring, likely

Aztec foundations: Aztlan, cities, peoples

considered by locals as a route to the underworld and the world of Tlalocan. Waters still flow from this spring in an easterly direction, and a small Christian shrine on the side of the pyramid has a well where modern-day pilgrims gather holy water. During its second phase, the Great Pyramid was aligned at 24–26 degrees north of west so that when the sun set behind Popocatepetl and Iztaccihuatl on the summer solstice, its rays illuminated a specific temple at the top—an epiphany that was visible throughout and beyond the city. Today an important Christian pilgrimage church dedicated to the Virgin of Remedies sits atop this great pyramid.

The worship of Quetzalcoatl, however, was not limited in any way to the Toltec site of Tula-Tollan; it played a major role for more than a thousand years in Cholula's religious and political life. A colonial official, an eyewitness to daily life in Cholula in the decades following the Spanish arrival, recalled that in the early mornings of festival days, groups of Cholula's citizens and pilgrims from other towns came to the ceremonial city carrying offerings of chickens, rabbits, quail, copal, perfume, fruit, and flowers. This wider reach of Cholula is reflected in the great diffusion of its distinctive ceramics and its shrines dedicated to deities of other communities.

All three great ceremonial capitals, predecessors to the "Great Tenochtitlan," contain monumental architecture imbued with mythic stories and religious symbolism serving as focal points for socially stratified communities ruled by sacred elites. When the Mexica arrived from Chicomoztoc and Aztlan into the Basin of Mexico, they encountered a long-standing urbanized way of life, which was organized by Toltec remnant city-states competing with each other for dominance over the ecological and social resources and surpluses of the region.

When social scientists realized the time depth and geographical spread of urbanism in Mesoamerican history, they also began to ask larger questions about other origins and evolutions, such as

when and how human beings first came into the Americas and
settled in the Basin of Mexico.

The origins of humans and society in the Americas

Long before there were debates about the nature of Aztec
urbanism, another fascinating question kept surfacing about the
historical origins of human populations in the Americas. Where
did the "Indians" of the newly discovered lands originally come
from? As reports, artifacts, and even Indians from the New World
were put on display in Spain, Portugal, and other European
countries, controversies broke out as to whether these peoples
were fully human, whether they descended from Adam and Eve,
and how they came to be located in these distant lands. The
answers given by priests, laypeople, and scholars fluctuated
between wonder, fantasy, and scientific hypotheses. The
sixteenth-century Italian-born historian of Spain, Peter Martyr
(Pietro Martire de Angheria) trumpeted to his readers, "Raise
your spirit, Hear about the New Discovery!" as news of Spanish
voyages of discovery poured into Europe. This was topped by
Francisco López de Gómara who, though he never traveled to the
New World, became Cortés's secretary in Spain and ranked the
"discovery" of the Americas as one of the three most important
events in human history, after the creation of the universe by God
and the life, death, and resurrection of Jesus Christ. When the
German painter Albrecht Dürer visited Brussels in 1520 to paint
a portrait of the king of Denmark, he saw an exhibition of the
Aztec treasure that Cortés had sent to the Holy Roman Emperor
Charles V. He waxed eloquently, "all the days of my life I have
seen nothing that rejoiced my heart so much as these things, for
I saw amongst them wonderful works of art, and I marveled at
the subtle genius of men in foreign lands. Indeed I cannot express
all that I thought there."

Back in Mexico, Diego Durán, a Dominican friar who spent
decades in Central Mexico barely a generation after the Aztec

capital fell, believed that ancient Christians had actually migrated from the Holy Land to Mexico. He thought that these Christian pilgrims had instilled certain key religious ideas in the local populace who, with time, forgot the true source and correct form of their devotional practices. He argued that either Saint Thomas or a lost tribe from Israel was the source of certain Aztec religious beliefs and practices, which to the Dominican looked very similar to Christian beliefs. Durán, who wrote three informative books about indigenous peoples and their ancient traditions in Central Mexico, hoped to one day find an ancient copy of the Holy Gospel in Hebrew, which he believed lay hidden in a native community near Mexico City. He did find a number of indigenous screenfold manuscripts, but unfortunately he did not preserve them.

The issue of where the Aztecs and their predecessors came from was linked to the question of whether these indigenous peoples had the sufficient intellect to create their own civilizations (what was later called the pattern of "independent invention") or needed sophisticated ideas, institutions, and practices imported from "superior" civilizations in the Old World.

One line of thought in the eighteenth century emphasized similarities between Aztec and Maya architecture and the pyramids in Egypt. This view held that the great achievements of the Egyptian pharaohs migrated out of the Mediterranean with ancient mariners, crossed the Atlantic Ocean, and were transplanted into Mexico millennia ago. Another view, expressed as early as 1804 by the German explorer Alexander von Humboldt, looked to the Pacific and suggested that Asian peoples migrated from China and Japan to the New World in ancient times, disseminating ideas, symbols, and ritual practices to the ancestors of the Aztecs and Toltecs. In the nineteenth century, American and European anthropologists debated whether the lost continent of Atlantis in the Atlantic or Mu in the Pacific could be the source of ancient American civilizations. Using Plato's description of the sinking of the legendary Atlantis, proponents of the submerged continent theory argued that the people who became the aboriginal Americans saved themselves in the nick of time and brought their great civilization to America.

In the twentieth century, the idea of transpacific contacts was explored by the anthropologist-adventurer Thor Heyerdahl, who constructed his raft *Kon-Tiki* and sailed across a section of the Pacific Ocean from Peru to the Polynesian islands, hoping to prove that pre-Hispanic peoples could have settled in Polynesia. Heyerdahl subsequently attempted to show that Mediterranean peoples could have made the journey to the Americas by sailing across the Atlantic, although his Egyptian-style reed boat *Ra* was actually designed and constructed by natives from the Lake Titicaca area of South America. Taking a cultural diffusionist approach, these interpretations argue that the achievements in the Americas were developed by migrating peoples who left centers of culture in the Old World and transplanted the roots of civilization (monumental architecture, writing, calendars, extensive market systems) to American soil. One serious problem with this notion is that not a single object from Asia, Africa, or the ancient Mediterranean has ever been found in any pre-Columbian archaeological context in the New World.

One eccentric view, the subject of several television specials, came from Erich von Däniken's book *Chariots of the Gods,* which argued that Maya and Aztec pyramids and sculptures as well as the Nazca Lines of Peru (huge geoglyphs etched in the desert) were left on earth by ancient cosmonauts whose extraterrestrial visits stimulated the development of, if not actually populated, the American continents. And von Däniken went to the extreme of suggesting that these great architectural structures were markers for the return of people from outer space at some future time.

More recently archaeologists, linguists, and molecular biologists using DNA evidence continue to struggle and identify when, from where, and by what routes the Americas were first populated.

While there is no universal agreement in answering these questions, a consensus has emerged that America was peopled by migrants from northeastern Asia who traveled by land and water perhaps as far back as 25,000 years ago. After rigorous analysis of various kinds of evidence it appears that the groups that entered the American landmass carried a number of distinctive cultural traditions during various migrations (through ice-free corridors) via the Bering Land Bridge linking Siberia to Alaska and the Northwest coast, and also by boat along these coastlines.

It is truly remarkable that the very first claim of this route appeared in *Historia natural y moral de las Indias* by Spanish Jesuit José de Acosta, published in Seville in 1590. Writing about the history of the Aztecs and Inca and noticing the similarity in physical appearance between American Indians and Asians, Acosta postulated that the civilizations of Mexico and Peru were built by people whose distant ancestors had migrated from Siberia several millennia before the Spaniards arrived. In sixteenth-century Europe no one had more than a vague sense of this northern landscape (the Danish explorer Vitus Bering discovered and named the Bering Strait in 1714), but Acosta pointed the way that scientists are still following in their efforts to pin down the routes, timing, and original homelands of the first migrants into the Americas.

Scholars now have clearly established that New World cultures, including the Mesoamerican civilizations that gave rise to the Aztecs and the Maya, developed as a result of cultural creativity and social interaction indigenous to the Americas. This is not to deny that impressive similarities between the Old and the New Worlds exist. But such similarities are no more impressive than the remarkable differences, innovations, and diversities among the cultural productions of Asia, the Mediterranean, Africa, and the Americas, and *within* the Americas as well. While it may be that some slight contact between Asian cultures and the peoples of the Americas took place, the Olmec, Huastec, Tlaxcalan,

Toltec, Ñuu Dzaui (Mixtec), Ñähñu (Otomí), Maya, Aztec, and all other indigenous cultures in the Western Hemisphere developed their own cultures independent of Old World civilizations. The urban endpoint of this long indigenous, evolutionary process took place in the Aztec capital of Tenochtitlan.

Chapter 3
Aztec expansion through conquest and trade

In spite of the deliberate destruction of Aztec pictorial documents by Spaniards in the early years after the fall of Tenochtitlan, a significant number of pre- and postconquest documents survive. Among them is an unusually beautiful codex, which was created by Aztec scribes in the early 1540s. Named after the Spanish viceroy who commissioned the work for his European emperor, the *Codex Mendoza* contains extraordinary images and descriptions of Aztec political, economic, and social history. The story and symbolism of this document, today housed in the Bodleian Library in Oxford, provides us with a useful guide to the bellicose career of Aztec kings and their achievements of political control over large territories and towns within and beyond the Basin of Mexico.

The *Codex Mendoza*

One of the leading patrons of the native artists was the first viceroy of New Spain, don Antonio de Mendoza, who was called a "Renaissance Maecenas" by one scholar in reference to the great patron of the arts in ancient Rome. Mendoza served as viceroy from 1535 to 1550, longer than any other, and when he arrived in Mexico City he found a world buffeted by indigenous uprisings, heated Spanish rivalries, and the destruction and extraction of native arts and documents ordered by the Crown to acquaint Emperor Charles V with New Spain. Mendoza invited trained artists and scribes, who were being schooled at the Franciscan college in Tlatelolco, to gather in a workshop where they could re-create the document that became the *Codex Mendoza*. It consists of seventy-one folios on Spanish paper, largely executed in the native style, with alphabetic glosses. The document is a rare example of how Mesoamericans and Europeans worked together to tell the Aztec story as a pictorial epic for royal eyes in a distant land. The native informants interpreting the pictograms and ideograms clearly argued over the meaning of some images, because the commentator who wrote the descriptions in Spanish noted that disagreements left him only ten days to complete the manuscript prior to the ship's departure for the king's court.

But this masterpiece was never seen by Charles V. The Spanish ship that carried it, along with other precious cargo, across the Atlantic was captured by French sailors who turned the codex over to the French court. Sometime before 1553, the *Codex Mendoza* came into the possession of André Thevet, the French royal cosmographer. Thevet was so excited by the document that he wrote his name and title on it five times, as if trying to make it his companion.

The document is divided into three sections, the first two of which appear to have been copied from no longer extant pre-Columbian originals: (1) the pre-Hispanic history of the Aztec capital of Tenochtitlan, beginning at the moment of its foundation and then recounting the explosive wars of conquest and expansion of its kings, including the two Motecuhzomas, through to the year 1523, (2) a colorful account of the various kinds of tribute paid to the capital between 1516 and 1518 by the nearly four hundred towns in five regions of the empire, and (3) a pictorial account of key aspects of the daily life, education, priestly training, crime and punishment, and social stratification of Mexica society.

Framed by time signs

The initial pictorial folio of the *Codex Mendoza* can be used as a window into the multiple realities of the Aztec world, including its calendars, agriculture, kingship, sacred spaces, mythology, ritual renewal, and human sacrifice. This single symmetrical illustration shows the last instant in the migration from Aztlan/Chicomoztoc and the first step toward empire. In the borders, calendar signs, in a series of blue boxes, frame the city and the significant acts depicted below it. Thevet's extravagant signature and title fill the gap at the top left. The year count (*xiuhpohualli*) almost always appears in Aztec pictorials, and here it begins at the top left with the sign for 2 House immediately to the left of the signature. This calendar continues down and around in a counterclockwise fashion mixing thirteen numbers, presented as dots, with the four year signs—House, Rabbit, Reed, and Flint Knife—and ends at the top with the year sign 13 Reed. The accompanying Spanish commentary states that "each little compartment...figured in blue...means one year." These fifty-one blocks almost make up the fifty-two-year Calendar Round, which, like our concept of century, marked a major time unit that renewed itself in the final year through a major public ritual.

A closer view reveals that there are indeed only fifty-one signs on the page and that the artists emphasized something special about the date 2 Reed, in the bottom right-hand corner. First, the date itself has a knot tied around it, signaling that a rare and powerful ritual called the "Binding of the Years" took place at that time. A fire-drill glyph with four puffs of smoke slightly to the side rises from the year sign, attached by a single thread, showing that this was the year of the New Fire Ceremony, one of the most profound ceremonies of the Mexica world. Once every fifty-two years at the culmination of the interlocking permutations of the 365-day solar calendar and the 260-day ritual calendar (an 18,980-day cycle), the spectacular New Fire Ceremony was held at the ceremonial site of the Hill of the Star, beyond the limits of the Aztec capital.

4. The founding of Tenochtitlan and the reign and early conquests of Tenuch, the first *tlatoani*, as painted on the frontispiece of the *Codex Mendoza*.

After destroying all household goods, extinguishing all home, temple, and community fires, and piercing and drawing blood from their children's ears, the populace waited in the darkness and watched for the passage of the constellation Tianquiztli (Marketplace), known to us as the Pleiades, through the celestial meridian. This moment of passage was marked by the lighting of the "new fire" on the chest of a sacrificed warrior who had marched out of Tenochtitlan earlier in the day among a huge entourage of musicians, priests, and members of the royal family. The single fire was then taken down the mountain into the center of the city and placed in the shrine of Huitzilopochtli, from which it was distributed to all parts of the empire. The artists who painted this symbol on the date 2 Reed were showing how time, with its orderly and sacred meanings, framed the early years of the capital city.

Chinampa agriculture

Within this temporal frame, the city appears as a large square with stylized blue borders representing the waters of Lake Tezcoco. Two intersecting blue lines, apparently representing canals, divide the island into four quarters. Within these four parts, we see a number of human, plant, and cultural images (a skull rack, a government building), which tell us about the Aztec city and its symbols. Spread throughout are signs of vegetation reflecting the agricultural life of the community.

These plants and waterways point to the impressive agricultural productivity of the Basin of Mexico. Called Anahuac by the Aztecs, the basin was a great natural saucer, covering more than 7,500 square miles, parts of which came to function as a productive breadbasket for the 1.2 million people living there. Aztec engineers transformed thousands of acres of poorly drained land into highly productive gardens in the fourteenth and fifteenth centuries. Through canal irrigation, swamp drainage, and the cultivation of maguey and nopal plants, the Aztec economy became so productive that it was able to support a population level that, after the arrival of the Spaniards and the onslaught of diseases and violence against the native peoples, was not reached again until the end of the nineteenth century.

Central to this explosive productivity were the *chinampas* (called "floating gardens" by the Spaniards) or raised agricultural beds, which fed a significant part of the Aztec population. *Chinampas* (derived from Nahuatl, meaning "surrounded by rushes") are plots of soil raised up on lake beds or freshwater swamps and shaped into long rectangular islets reinforced by rushes, branches, logs, and other organic materials. The porosity of the soil and the continual flow of water through the narrow canals insured constant fertilization of the soils and plants, and created an environment filled with aquatic birds, fish, insects, algae, and frogs.

The enormous Basin of Mexico was an internal drainage system surrounded on all sides by hills, piedmonts, and high mountains. The result at the lowest elevations was a group of extensive shallow, swampy areas and interconnected lakes covering more than four hundred square miles. It was onto one of these swampy islands that the Aztecs were driven when they enraged the ruler of Colhuacan upon sacrificing his daughter. In a rags-to-riches scenario the Aztecs soon transformed the swamps into a world of nutritious and tasty foods. Bernal Díaz del Castillo thus reported about his visit to the great Aztec market at Tlatelolco: "Let us go on and speak of those who sold beans and sage and other vegetables and herbs in another part of the market, and let us also mention the fruiters, and the women who sold cooked food, dough, and tripe in their own part of the market." Bernardino de Sahagún's native informants gave long lists of plants and foodstuffs including many varieties of maize, beans, amaranth, chia, chilies, tomatoes, and fruit.

Though there is no *chinampa* in the *Codex Mendoza* image, its presence is reflected there in the various healthy looking plants that dot the four parts of the city landscape. It is clear that the composers of the *Codex Mendoza* were signaling to the viewer, especially through the blooming cactus in the central space, that plants and cultivation were crucial to their existence, mythology, and economic life.

Rulers: the *tlatoani*

Around the arresting central image of the *Codex Mendoza* frontispiece and distributed throughout the four quadrants of the city sit ten males, nine identically dressed and one more prominently attired, who represent Mexica leaders. In this distribution and difference we are introduced to one of the signal features of Mexica society: intensive social stratification and the powers of the ruler. Nine of these men appear with a white *tilmatli* (robe) snugly wrapped around their bodies; they are seated on bundles of green reeds with their hair worn in the warrior style known as *temillotl* (pillar of stone), signifying their achievements as warriors. The tenth man in the *Codex Mendoza* image is the most prominent leader. He is distinguished by a blue speech glyph in front of his mouth signifying that he is the *tlatoani* or chief speaker. His elevation above the others is further marked by his black body paint (signifying his priestly status), smears of blood on his temple and right ear, indicating his bloodletting rites, and loosely tied hair, showing that he was a priest.

His name is expressed by the thin line attached to the sign above and behind him, which is a blooming cactus growing from a stylized rock, a symbolic duality reflecting the central image that supports the giant eagle. This name glyph translates as Tenuch (Stone-Cactus-Fruit), written on the front of his white garment. This part of the painting gives us the important information that the supreme human authority in Aztec Mexico resided in the imperial capital of Tenochtitlan and was closely identified with the eagle-cactus-water imagery in the center.

Aztec rulers as warrior kings

Aztec rulers had to distinguish themselves in warfare as commanders in order to fulfill their religious, social, and economic duties. A great king conquered many towns, which increased rich tributary payments to the royal and capital storehouses. It is believed that one Aztec ruler, Tizoc, whose military expansions were meager, was assassinated by members of the royal household for his weak leadership. This emphasis on warfare as a tool of the expansion of imperial control by the Mexica is vividly shown in the bottom section of the *Codex Mendoza* image where giant warriors conquer two towns on the mainland. Away from the city, on the other side of the waterways but still within the time frame of the fifty-one year signs, the Mexica under the rulership of Tenuch (1325–77) carry out conquests against the communities of Colhuacan (Curved Hill) and Tenayuca (Rampart Hill), both of which were located outside the city. The standard glyph in the codex for the conquest of a community is a tipped and burning temple that signifies that the structure, symbols, gods, energy, and "essences" of a community have been defeated.

The expression of Mexica dominance is illustrated by the posture, costumes, and especially the size of the warriors. The two Mexica warriors wear the standard Aztec armor of thick quilted cotton. They wear their hair in the pillar-of-stone style and carry the *ihuiteteyo* shield, symbolizing the city. They not only dwarf the enemy warriors but symbolically subdue them by pressing their shields down onto their heads to force them to crouch. The Aztec warrior may also be gripping, behind the shield, the *temilotl* (the sacred forelock) of the enemy as an act of ritual dominance. In Aztec thought, grasping another's *temilotl* was equivalent to capturing the *tonalli*, one of the essences or souls of the enemy.

The temple imagery shows war as an action with religious meanings crucial to the foundation and expansion of Tenochtitlan.

Historically, the rise of the Aztec capital and tributary empire began in the early decades of the fourteenth century when they walked into a world of warring city-states that populated the Basin of Mexico. The basic political unit was a city or *altepetl*, which ruled a kingdom or *tlatocayotl*, each with a *tlatoani* chosen by the sons and grandsons of the previous ruler. Each kingdom included dependent communities that worked the agricultural lands, paid tribute, and performed services for the elite classes in the capital according to various ritual calendars and cosmological patterns. Let us now turn to the royal careers of the Aztec rulers to trace their rise to dominance in central Mesoamerica.

Royal families of warrior kings

The history of Aztec kings involves enormous family ambitions, palace intrigue and assassination, military genius and religious devotion, great wealth, and gift-giving to win loyal nobles. All Aztec rulers shared the same lineage that combined humbler Chichimec origins with the revered Toltec tradition associated with the great priest-king Quetzalcoatl, which linked their authority to celestial deities of wisdom and war. After Tenuch came Acamapichtli (1377–97), whose name glyph consists of a hand grasping a bundle of reed arrows. His ascent to the throne established Aztec political legitimacy in the Basin of Mexico by tying them closely to the royal house at Azcapotzalco, the capital of the dominant Tepanec kingdom where the iron-fisted Tezozomoc reigned. The symbol of Acamapichtli's name is an appropriate indicator of the goals and practices of all Aztec rulers. Each was a warrior king whose purpose was to grasp and control territory, and expand tribute payments and political allegiances. Reeds had religious meanings signifying divinely inspired fertility, renewal of the cosmos, and access to the gods.

As the son of a Mexica nobleman and a princess from the Toltec lineage, Acamapichtli created a period of stability and successful warfare. He had twenty-one wives and was remembered more than a century later for his progeny of warrior chiefs who helped the Aztecs in their rise to empire. In his effective building campaign, the Aztecs constructed royal houses, *chinampas*, and canals that began to give heft and order to the island city. He led the conquest of four important towns in the southern part of the basin and helped organize an early version of what came to be known as a "flowery war" with Chalco, a town on the southern edge of the lakes that, up until the time the Spaniards arrived, maintained a powerful rivalry and resistance against Tenochtitlan. The flowery wars were a type of "war game" whose purpose was not so much to conquer territory as it was to provide a training ground for warriors and a source for gaining sacrificial captives.

Acamapichtli was followed by one of his sons, Huitzilihuitl (Hummingbird Feather, 1397–1420), who doubled his father's conquests and strengthened the Mexica ties to the supreme city-state of Azcapotzalco when he married the granddaughter of its mighty king Tezozomoc *after* marrying the princess of the powerful city-state of Tlacopan. These unions proved to be highly beneficial for the growing Aztec city-state as three of his children—Chimalpopoca, Motecuhzoma Ilhuicamina, and the great and dreaded statesman Tlacaelel (each from a different mother)—became potent leaders during the middle years of Aztec expansion. Huitzilihuitl advanced the art of sacred rulership, using his growing status as a man-god to command the building of important temples, establish laws, and initiate ritual practices that performed the myths of his ancestors. His prestige was heightened when the New Fire Ceremony, celebrated during his reign, identified him as a ruler with cosmic powers to revitalize the universe.

It was during the reign of his son, Chimalpopoca (Smoking Shield, 1417–27) that Mexica political fortunes faced an enormous crisis in their relationship with the Tepanec empire and its royal family. Chimalpopoca was the favored grandson of Tezozomoc, whose affection for the young Mexica ruler translated into reduced tribute payments from Tenochtitlan to the Tepanec capital. Housing conditions improved, and supplies from the nearby market town of Tlatelolco provided better and more diverse foodstuffs and craft goods. Although modest conquests were carried out during his reign, the political world took a darker turn when Tezozomoc's death in 1426 resulted in a vicious power struggle between his sons, Maxtla and Tayueh. Chimalpopoca supported Tayueh, who lost the battle against his brother. According to some sources, Maxtla captured Chimalpopoca and humiliated him by imprisoning him in a cage before assassinating him. In the face of this political crisis, the Mexica turned to the more mature forty-six-year-old Itzcoatl (Obsidian Serpent) to serve as their next ruler. He turned the tide in the Mexica favor during his reign from 1428 to 1440.

Itzcoatl was aided by two experienced assistants, his nephew Motecuhzoma Ilhuicamina and the skilled Mexica politician Tlacaelel, which enabled him to lead the most important revolution in Aztec history and guide a military expansion of territories that defined the future of the Aztec empire. Realizing that the Tepanec empire could be defeated, Itzcoatl organized a well-planned rebellion that shifted lands, power, allegiances, and tribute away from Azcapotzalco. According to one tradition, he did so through a potent alliance with the commoners of the rebellious towns. When a dissident Mexica faction, fearful of Tepanec reprisals if they lost, threatened to break away from the rebellion, Tlacaelel engineered a remarkable agreement. Fight with us, he urged, and if we lose, we the Aztec nobles will be your servants. If we win, you will serve us in a new kingdom and enjoy the well-being that will come. Then the Tepanec town of Tlacopan and the forces from Tezcoco, ruled by the daring and brilliant Nezahualcoyotl (Hungry Coyote), joined the Mexica, and together they destroyed Maxtla's forces and power.

Immediately the rulers of Tenochtitlan, Tlacopan, and Tezcoco formed an *excan tlatoloyan* or Tribunal of Three Places, which became the foundation of the budding empire. This military confederation, known as the Triple Alliance, began a nearly one-hundred-year hegemonic expansion through conquest and tribute control of communities subjugated by treaty or warfare. Over time, Mexico-Tenochtitlan became by far the dominant city in the Tribunal of Three Places. In one surviving codex, we see that Itzcoatl's armies conquered twenty-four major towns and city-states that stretched from the central plateau to previously unconquered towns in Guerrero to the south.

Itzcoatl managed another social revolution, this one internal. He confiscated and burned the libraries of commoners because, in the view of his priests, these codices contained false religious teachings and histories. The royal religion celebrating Huitzilopochtli, Quetzalcoatl, and Tezcatlipoca would face no competition from local shamans and commoner priests who preached the worship of other gods. Itzcoatl increased tribute payments to military heroes and established a strict dress code for ranks of warriors.

When Itzcoatl died in 1440 his nephew Motecuhzoma Ilhuicamina (1441–69) came to the throne with unprecedented experience in warfare and social leadership. This first Motecuhzoma (his grandson Motecuhzoma Xocoyotzin was the ruler when the Spaniards arrived in 1519) had been a member of the Council of Four and the commanding general of Mexica forces during the revolution against Azcapotzalco. The *Codex Mendoza* states that he was "very serious, severe, and virtuous, ... of good temper and judgment, and an enemy of evil." The social and political boundaries of the Aztec empire greatly expanded during his reign and led to an enormous increase in tribute for the Triple Alliance. He ordered the construction of new religious and political edifices within the city, and the Great Temple itself underwent a sizable expansion. When this ruler held lavish public ceremonies in which the ritual sacrifices of humans and animals increased to new levels, his prestige as a divine personage also grew.

He used this sacred prestige to divide his society internally so that the commoner class (*macehualtin*) were forced into legal subservience to the noble class (*pipiltin*). The nobles became exempt from paying tribute to the rulers and were ensured the best education so they could rise to the professions of judges, administrators, and philosophers. The *macehualtin* were required to pay tribute in the forms of goods and labor, especially in the construction of public buildings. Below them all were the slaves (*tlatlacotin*), who were forced into strict servitude for failing to pay debts or other legal violations. The *tlatlacotin* kept their property and family while working off their penalties and could be restored to their previous social status. But those who failed to satisfy their obligations could become "collar slaves" who could be sold and eventually sacrificed.

Even while the Aztec state was expanding in multiple ways, several disasters struck at the crucial economic system. In 1446 a huge locust plague weakened crop yields throughout the basin. Then in 1449 floods inundated parts of the island city, interrupting social life, agricultural production, and ritual performance, and challenging the community's faith in its gods and leadership. Motecuhzoma commissioned his allied ruler in the Triple Alliance, Nezahualcoyotl in Tezcoco, to build a massive dike to control flood waters from ruining *chinampas* and neighborhoods. Then a greater threat appeared in the form of a four-year famine. Many Aztecs had to sell themselves into slavery in distant and better-fed areas of the empire, especially in the "hot lands" of the Gulf Coast tributary regions. When the rains returned in 1454, there was widespread relief and religious celebrations to thank the gods.

As the imperial family and its military units carved out new territories for the Aztec empire, they encountered several powerful military barriers they could never completely overcome. Beyond the eastern side of the Basin of Mexico stood the Tlaxcalan kingdom, which had its own tributary towns, powerful warrior societies, and shrewd rulers. It was this kingdom that was to form the crucial alliance with the Spaniards when they arrived, turning the Spanish assault into as much an indigenous rebellion as a European conquest. On the western frontier stood the independent Tarascan kingdom that would soon prove just how weak the Aztecs could be when they strayed too far from their central territories.

When Motecuhzoma Ilhuicamina died in 1469, a greenhorn ruler by the name of Axayacatl (Face of Water) rose to the throne. The son of Motecuhzoma and grandson of Itzcoatl, he was carefully tutored by the master politician Tlacaelel as he soon faced threats from the edge of the empire where Mexica governors were assassinated by rebellious communities. The leading rebel community was Cuextlaxtlan, which became the target of Aztec wrath in the form of a brutal attack and imposition of twice the tributary payments as before.

While arranging a number of alliances through his many wives, Axayacatl also sired two future rulers of the Aztec empire, Motecuhzoma Xocoyotzin and Cuitlahuac, who occupied the throne briefly during the war of Spanish conquest. His biggest threat, however, came from nearby. For some years prior to his rule, the island city of Tlatelolco, just a few kilometers from Tenochtitlan, had grown into a major market center and maintained a tense rivalry with the growing Aztec capital. The ruler of Tlatelolco, Moquihuix, chose to defy Axayacatl's rule and demands for more access to Tlatelolco's market system. One Aztec source reflecting the hometown view states that the lord of Tlatelolco was a powerful and haughty ruler who provoked Axayacatl into a battle. Moquihuix fled into the main temple to avoid being taken prisoner but was rebuked by a priest for cowardice. Apparently he flung himself from a high temple and died on the steps below. Axayacatl's victory in this conflict brought Tlatelolco and its great marketplace firmly under Tenochtitlan's control.

This Aztec ruler conquered thirty-seven towns according to the *Codex Mendoza*, but he also suffered a humiliating defeat when he led an ill-fated campaign against the western kingdom of the Tarascans. The Aztecs were striving to build a solid buffer zone between themselves and the independent Tarascan empire, so they conquered the various towns that bordered the two kingdoms. But Axayacatl went too far. In the subsequent campaign against the Tarascans, who significantly outnumbered the Aztec military units now fighting a long way from home, Axacayatl's warriors were crushed, and they retreated to Tenochtitlan in humiliation. This was the first real sign of Aztec limits, one that would haunt them in the coming decades as periodic chinks in their military armor began to show in various regions.

When Axacayatl died in 1481, his younger brother Tizoc took the throne and managed the least productive and shortest reign of any Aztec ruler. Nevertheless, his fifteen conquests as well as the Aztec understanding of the linkage between cosmology and warfare are magnificently portrayed in one of the greatest of Aztec sculptures, the Tizoc Stone. Like many Aztec sculptures, this imperial monument depicts human life as situated within a celestial context and warfare as a ritual practice taking place and renewing human life between the cosmo-magical forces of heaven and earth. A solar disk and a band of stars representing the celestial roof of the world covers the top and the upper register of the side of the stone. A band on the lower register depicts upright pointed blades and four masks of the earth deity, representing the terrestrial level where humans suffer sacrifice and certain death. Between these celestial and terrestrial levels, a parade of fourteen upright Mexica warriors in full regalia grasp the scalp locks of the submitting deities of conquered towns. In the center of this series of conquests stands the ruler Tizoc himself, dressed as the potent Aztec deities Huizilopochtli and Tezcatlipoca. The entire sculpture presents the world as a sacred circle organized by Aztec conquests as ritual practices that secure Tenochtitlan and its ruler as the spatial and human centers of the world.

Other surviving historical sources suggest a very different history of Tizoc's conquests as largely conquests of rebellious towns and that he was not able to expand the territory of the Aztec empire as his predecessors had so ably done. It appears that he was assassinated by order of the Council of Four who arranged for him to be poisoned.

This troublesome lull in the processes of Aztec expansions of lands and tribute was powerfully reversed when Tizoc's younger brother Ahuitzotl began his sixteen-year reign in 1486. The most effective of Aztec warrior kings, he expanded the state into an empire that reached from coast to coast and added a new level of splendor to the rites and lifestyle of the royal household where it was said, "the music never ceased, day or night." This taste for sumptuous display extended to the imperial ritual performances held at the Great Aztec Temple. From his coronation ceremony to the end of his reign, Ahuitzotl elevated the scale and pomp of building and sacrificial ceremonies to new heights. During his rule the long-distance merchants known as the *pochteca* acquired greater amounts of tribute from distant communities, including the lands of Soconusco on the far southern coast.

Recent archaeological excavations have abundantly shown that the Aztec royal family made the care, expansion, and ritual life of the Great Temple its most important symbolic business. It was periodically enlarged through extravagant spectacles of dancing, praying, blood sacrifices, presentations of sculptures, and gift-giving to nobles. Major events in the life of the state or the careers of Aztecs were marked by great public ceremonies, and Ahuitzotl built on this tradition with great aplomb. In 1487

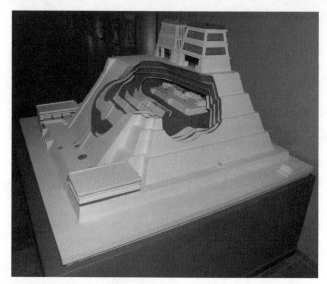

5. Model depicting the various successive, twin-structured rebuildings of the Great Aztec Temple that served as a container of offerings from throughout the empire.

Ahuitzotl chose to enlarge the Great Temple and, under the inspiration of his warrior gods, carried out the most brutal public display of human sacrifices in the history of Tenochtitlan. The political nature of Ahuitzotl's ritual extravaganza was marked by transporting the leaders from towns he had conquered and forcing them to watch, from behind screens, the deaths of their own warriors. It is said they returned to their communities full of fear.

One of the most astonishing structures these visitors saw was the huge *tzompantli* (skull rack) that stood near the Great Temple. Returning for a moment to our image of Tenochtitlan in the *Codex Mendoza*, we see a drawing of the skull rack immediately to the right of the giant eagle and the blooming cactus. In Aztec shrines, racks were loaded with the skulls of sacrificial victims symbolizing the Aztec acquisition of the spiritual force of the enemy warriors captured in combat and beheaded in the capital. When the Spaniards arrived in Mesoamerica thirty years after Ahuitzotl's extravagant ceremonies, they reported seeing numerous skull racks holding thousands of skulls. Aztec sculptors built an intimidating skull temple, immediately to the side of the Great Temple, made up of scores of skulls carved in stone, representing military conquests on earth and the presence of Mictlan, the underworld, in the heart of their sacred precinct. Whatever else he accomplished in his forty-five conquests, Ahuitzotl managed to elevate the prestige of the office of the *tlatoani* to that of a divine-warrior-hero-king, the living incarnation of Huitzilopochtli, who was triumphantly seated at the top of the Great Temple. Because Ahuitzotl had spent so much of his military power on the borderlands and peripheries of the realm, the Aztec empire was larger than ever and now seemed to be solidly balanced at the capital. But it still was vulnerable to rebellion and broken alliances.

The most legendary of Aztec kings was Motecuhzoma Xocoyotzin, the revered Motecuhzoma the Younger, who ruled from 1502 until his death while a hostage of Cortés in 1520. Though we know more about his appearance, attitudes, and life than of any other Aztec ruler, he remains the most enigmatic of them all. On the one hand, he was highly successful as a military commander and ritual leader, while on the other, his actions during the Spanish assault suggest a vulnerable, pensive, and hesitant ruler unable to read the political signs of the Spanish danger. The son of Axayacatl and nephew of Ahuitzotl, he came to the throne at the age of thirty-four after a distinguished career as a military commander and political leader during the years of the great expansion of his predecessor. He reconquered and consolidated parts of the empire while he enhanced the prestige and wealth of his nobles in Tenochtitlan, thereby assuring their allegiance to his throne. Motecuhzoma's extravagant lifestyle included taking many wives—one account mentions more than two hundred. These

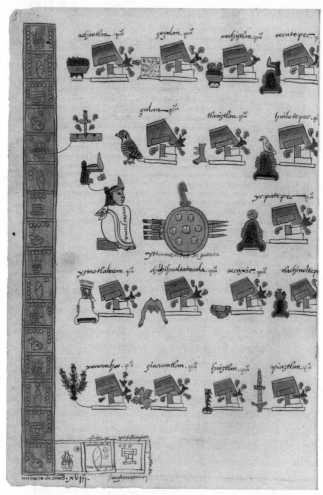

6. Motecuhzoma Xocoyotzin, the ninth *tlatoani* of Tenochtitlan who reigned from 1502 to 1520, depicted with sixteen of his forty-four conquests.

marriages were, in part, political arrangements that strengthened the ability of the Mexica to form and maintain military and economic alliances with nearby and distant city-states. They also resulted in a large number of children who became members of his royal entourage and government. Díaz del Castillo tells us that the emperor was neat, clean, slender, tall, and well built. We also read that when he had sex with his many wives he did so quietly! Cortés, in his letters to the king of Spain, described the life of the court: Apparently, every day at sunrise, more than five hundred noblemen and their attendants would arrive at Motecuhzoma's palace and spend the day walking, talking, meeting, and planning governmental events. Hundreds of servants would fill the courtyards and streets near the palace.

In the last decade of his reign, he attempted without success to subdue the rival kingdoms of Tlaxcala and Huexotzingo to the east. Four futile wars and numerous "flowery wars" resulted in a profound hostility between the Aztecs and the Tlaxcalans. This entrenched enmity became absolutely crucial in enabling the Spaniards to bring a devastating end to the line of *tlatoque* created when the ruler whose name symbolized the grasping of territories and sacred plants took the throne almost 150 years before.

By the time that Díaz del Castillo and his comrades were given their tour of Tenochtitlan during that first fateful week after their arrival in 1519, the Aztec *tlatoani* Motecuhzoma Xocoyotzin was surrounded by an elaborate court dedicated to enhancing his sacred authority through spectacle and splendor. According to Cortés's second letter to the king of Spain, Motecuhzoma changed clothes four times a day, never putting on garments that he had previously worn.

An empire of trade

The Aztec merchants were empire builders, too. They built an empire of trade. Historians have shown that the Aztec world was more fully integrated economically than it was politically. By the time the second Motecuhzoma came to power in 1502, the empire was divided into thirty districts. Different kinds of tribute were collected on a careful schedule and brought into the Basin of Mexico to the central markets and especially the royal palaces. A traveler in the Aztec world in 1500 would have witnessed eight provinces that paid huge amounts of tribute to the Triple Alliance as food and luxury goods poured into numerous open-air markets where potters, basket makers, lapidaries, and other craft specialists exchanged their products every five days among neighbors and people passing through. Larger settlements had daily markets, and Tlatelolco was so filled with people that it was said the din of their conversation, storytelling, and bickering before the judges could be heard a mile away.

The merchant classes of the Aztec empire had their own hierarchy based on their experience, regions where they worked, and success of their accomplishments. Itinerant regional merchants known as *tlanecuilo* managed a market circuit through the exchange of maize, chili, baskets, gourd bowls, turkeys, salt, cotton, and the all-important cacao. Crucial to the importation and exchange culture of the Aztecs, as well as to its political expansion toward ever moving peripheries, were the *pochteca*, the merchants who traveled long distances to trade on their own but also to spy, make war, and bring goods home to the rulers. They had groups of porters at their command and managed the transportation of obsidian knives and jewelry, beautifully decorated cloths, dyes, jade, turquoise, tropical bird feathers, warrior costumes, and sometimes slaves. In one case, the town of Tochtepec on the eastern Gulf Coast provided 16,000 rubber balls to be used in the ritual ballgames played in the core area of the empire.

Merchants were part of a frontier communication system and crucial in the collection of war booty. When wars were successful, the mopping-up operation was led by the *pochteca*, who went in and assessed the goods, supplies, and production capabilities of the conquered town so that the appropriate level of tribute could be registered. In fact, the *tlatoani* Ahuitzotl had taken great pains to set up an effective communication system with returning merchants to ensure that the war booty was quickly brought into his royal market. The ruler's prestige increased from his timely ability to redistribute the goods, some of which went to the returning merchants as payment for their extremely hard work.

The dangers and hardships of these carriers of goods cannot be exaggerated. They left home, went out into hostile terrain, and skirted enemy communities. They journeyed through perilous gorges, scaled steep hills and mountains, crossed treacherous rivers, and risked exposure to ritual pollution. They operated in the fear that they would hear the cry of the *huactli* or "laughing falcon," which could signify their doom. If the falcon laughed for a short time during their journey, it was considered a good omen, and success was ensured. But when "they heard that it laughed too long, in a high pitch, as if its bosom and side tightened; or as if it screamed swollen with joy... they felt that perhaps something woeful would now betide them; they would come upon something perilous." Their labors were considered heroic, and when successful they brought riches and honor to their ruler, the city, and themselves.

As with all parts of Aztec society, the work of the merchants was intertwined with ritual activities, specific deities, and even human sacrifices, which they called "debt-payments." When merchants departed their home community, their journeys were dictated by favorable day signs in the calendar. These especially included 1 Serpent, ironically called "the straight way," but also the days 2 Crocodile, 1 Monkey, and 7 Serpent. To launch the expedition, a ceremonial feast was organized by the vanguard merchant and attended by family and friends. Elder merchants and parents delivered speeches filled with the lore and lessons of the trading life. This was followed by the decoration of their merchant's staff with the symbol and image of their god, using cut papers and liquid rubber. "They gave it lips, nose, eyes. It resembled a man. Thus did they make a representation of the fire god." Some transformed their walking staffs into god images of Tlaltecuhtli (the earth deity) or Yacatecuhtli (the patron god of merchants), as these staffs were the magical guides and protectors of the merchants.

Often, returning merchants brought the painful news of attacks, sickness, and death on the road. The elders put the returning merchants through a harsh interrogation about the facts of the expedition, ambushes, meetings, exchanges, and the intensity of their work. Drinking and feasting followed, and the goods were taken to the *tlatoani*, whose assistants recorded them and arranged for their distribution according to the desires of the ruler.

Chapter 4
Cosmovision and human sacrifice

No topic has caused more controversy and confusion about Aztec life than human sacrifice. Chroniclers, priests, anthropologists, journalists, filmmakers, and creative writers have repeatedly focused on it, some to condemn it, some to refute it ever took place, and some to understand the indigenous purposes and cultural meanings of ritual killing and the ritual ingestion of human flesh. That the Aztecs practiced ritual human sacrifice is beyond doubt, but it is also clear that Spanish chroniclers exaggerated the numbers and purposes of these sacrifices as a strategy to justify their own conquests and prodigious violence against Mesoamerican men, women, and children. Scholarship also reveals that many ancient cultures including the Romans, Greeks, Japanese, Chinese, Africans, Andeans, and Egyptians practiced human sacrifice, often in very large numbers. Even though the Aztec image in Western thought ranks them as the biggest sacrificers in the world, there is no substantial archaeological or documentary proof that they ritually killed more people than other civilizations.

Evidence of human sacrifice

During the height of the battle between Spaniards and Aztecs for control of Tenochtitlan, Bernal Díaz del Castillo described seeing his comrades being forcibly dragged up the steps of the

Great Temple by Aztec warriors and priests. As the "dismal drum" of the war god droned above the scene, mixed with the ominous sounds of shell and horn trumpets, the Aztecs decorated their captives with ritual costumes and "with fans in their hands they forced them to dance before" Huitzilopochtli. The Aztecs pushed them onto their backs on an altar and with sacrificial knives cut open their chests and drew out their palpitating hearts, then "offered them to the idols that were there." To his fear and horror, Díaz del Castillo saw them roll the bodies down the steep steps of the Great Temple to land, broken, at the bottom. He tells us that they "cut off their arms and feet and flayed the skin off the faces, and prepared it afterwards like glove leather with the beards on, and kept those for the festivals when they celebrated drunken orgies and the flesh they ate in *chilmole*."

This kind of eyewitness observation can be combined with Aztec pictorial and alphabetic sources, the detailed accounts of elders interviewed by Spanish friars, as well as archaeological evidence, to show that ritual violence was a basic part of Aztec life. We now know that ritual killing long predates the Aztecs with the earliest Mesoamerican evidence coming from hunter-gatherers in the Tehuacán Valley at around 5000 BCE. It is also likely that many city-states before the Aztecs practiced some form of human sacrifice. But there is a huge discrepancy between the numbers that the Spanish "eyewitnesses" tell us and what careful archaeological work in this area has revealed. For instance, here is what the record shows at the Great Temple of Tenochtitlan, the most thoroughly excavated Aztec site in Mesoamerica, where the largest numbers of sacrifices most likely took place:

- Two sacrificial stones (*techcatl*) stood at the entrance to the two shrines at the top of the Great Temple. Each rose from the floor about 50 centimeters and served as altars for ritual killings, just as Díaz del Castillo described them.

- More than a thousand ritual knives, mainly of flint, were uncovered in the excavation of different stages and offering caches. They are carefully decorated and often transformed into the face of a deity awaiting the sacrificial moment. Evidence shows that these knives were not used in the ritual killings but rather were symbolic offerings.
- Traces on the surfaces of statues, altars, and floors of certain ritual chambers reveal that sacrificial blood was smeared on divine images and spilled in significant quantities.
- The human remains of 126 people were buried throughout the site. Forty-two are children who, suffering from various diseases, had their throats slit so the blood could be used as an offering to the gods. Forty-seven adult heads with the top vertebrae connected were found in various offerings. Only three complete human skulls have been uncovered. They were perforated at the temples probably indicating that they had previously hung on a nearby skull rack. Thirty-three facial skull masks decorated with shell-and-pyrite eyes and representing the Lord of the Underworld, Mictlantecuhtli, were deposited in the floors of the Great Temple.

This is the sum total of all sacrificial human remains found in over thirty seasons of intensive excavations in the main ritual precinct of Tenochtitlan. It is remarkable that more human remains have been found at the site of Teotihuacan (1–550 CE) than at this central ritual landscape and capital of the Aztec empire. A Spanish account claims that more than 80,000 enemy warriors were sacrificed in a four-day ceremony, and yet no evidence approaching one-hundredth of that number has been found in the excavations of Tenochtitlan.

Sacrifice and cosmovision

The reliable documentary evidence found in the writings of Bernardino de Sahagún based on extensive interviews with Aztec elders in the decades after the fall of Tenochtitlan nevertheless tells us that sacrifices took place every month at various temples and altars in the ceremonial centers. The Aztecs carried out human sacrifice within a larger, more complex ceremonial system in which a tremendous amount of energy, wealth, and time was spent in a variety of festivals dedicated to a crowded and hungry pantheon of divine entities. This ritual dedication is reflected in the many metaphors and symbols related to war and sacrifice. Human hearts were likened to fine burnished turquoise, and war was referred to as *teoatltlachinolli* (divine liquid and burnt things),"where the jaguars roar," where "feathered war bonnets heave about like foam in the waves." Death on the battlefield was called *xochimiquiztli* (flowery death), reminiscent of the modern claim that it is "good and noble to die for one's country."

The greatest ceremonial precinct where the majority of sacrifices took place formed the architectural axis of Tenochtitlan and each of its four sides measured 440 meters. It contained more than eighty temples, skull racks, schools, and other structures. Book 2 of Sahagún's *Florentine Codex* provides a valuable list of most of these buildings, including the Great Temple, which stood "in the middle of the square,... very large, very tall,... and ... faced toward the setting of the sun." We also read of a temple where "Motecuhzoma did penances,... there was dying there; captives died there." There was Mexico Calmecac, the main high school of the city, where "dwelt the penitents who offered incense at the summit of the pyramid Temple of Tlaloc. This they did quite daily." There was a temple from which men were thrown into fires and burned to death. Nearby stood the Great Skull Rack, where the heads of sacrificial victims were hung for display. Another temple was dedicated to the corn goddess, where a young woman impersonating the goddess 7 Snake was sacrificed at night. "And when she died, then they flayed her,... the fire priest put on the skin." Another temple related to cooking and eating human flesh was described where "they gathered together the sacrificial victims called Tlalocs,... when they had slain them, they cut them to pieces there and cooked them. They put squash blossoms with their flesh,... then the noblemen ate them, all the high judges; but not the common folk—only the rulers."

Although important variations of ritual activity were carried out at these temples, schools, skull racks, and elsewhere, the general pattern began with *nezahualiztli*, a preparatory period of fasting, usually lasting four (or a multiple of four) days. An important exception was the year-long partial fast by a group of priests and priestesses known as "god-eaters" or the greatly feared "elder brothers of Huitzilopochtli who fasted for a year." This preparatory period also involved nocturnal vigils and offerings of flowers, food, cloth, rubber, paper, and poles with streamers, as well as incensing, the pouring of libations, and the embowering of temples, statues, and ritual participants. Dramatic processions of elaborately costumed individuals, moving to music ensembles and playing sacred songs, passed through the ceremonial precinct before arriving at the specific temple of sacrifice. The people who were to be sacrificed were called *teteo ixiptla* (deity impersonators).

It may come as a surprise that the most common form of sacrifice was autosacrifice. This involved the use of maguey thorns or other sharp instruments to pierce one's earlobes, thighs, arms, tongue, or, in the case of sinners and priests, genitals, in order to offer blood to the gods. The most common type of killing was the beheading of animals like the quail. But the most dramatic and valued sacrifices were those of captured warriors, women, children, and slaves. These victims were ritually bathed, carefully costumed, often taught special dances, and sometimes either fattened or slimmed down during the preparation period. In one of the most fascinating examples, during the feast of Toxcatl, great care was taken to choose a male with the most perfect body who would ritually become the prodigious god Tezcatlipoca before he was sacrificed. This perfect body had to be

> like something smoothed, like a tomato, like a pebble, as if sculpted in wood; he was not curly haired,... not rough of forehead,... not long-headed,... not of swollen eyelids,... not of downcast face; he was not flat-nosed;... he was not concave nosed,... he was not

thick-lipped, he was not gross-lipped, he was not a stutterer,...not buck-toothed...His teeth were like seashells,...he was not tomato-eyed...He was not long-handed, he was not fat-gingered,... he was not of protruding navel; he was not of hatchet shaped buttocks...For him who had no flaw, who had no defects, who had no blemish, who had no mark,...there was taken the greatest care that he be taught to blow the flute, that he be able to play his whistle. And that at the same time he holds all his flowers and his smoking tube.

Moreover, this person lived in luxury for an entire year as he promenaded, with guards, throughout the city, playing his flute, greeting people in gracious prose, for he was the living image of one of the most powerful of Aztec gods.

About thirty years ago, a heated debate broke out in academic and popular journals about the extent and purpose of Aztec cannibalism. Some argued that the Aztecs ate large numbers of people as a necessary source of protein. The Aztec state was called the "Cannibal Kingdom" by an anthropologist who unfortunately did a very limited study of the evidence. The opponents of the protein argument stated that cannibalism in Aztec Mexico was primarily a ritual need to feed the gods and renew their energy, not a gastronomic need of humans to feed themselves. This meant that in the Aztec understanding of sacrifice and cannibalism, it was the gods who were nurtured through the ritual offerings of blood and human flesh. The Aztecs had abundant protein sources in their environment, thus only small amounts of human flesh were consumed, primarily by nobles, on relatively rare occasions.

Worldview and sacrifice

The ritual practice of human sacrifice is closely connected to the shape and rhythms of Aztec worldview or cosmovision, which posited two distinguishable parts of the universe: the space-time of the gods and the space-time of the creatures of this world that the gods created. Human beings, animals, plants, celestial objects, minerals, and rain occupied this visible space-time world that divine beings penetrated through *malinalli*, or double-helix-shaped portals located in trees, creeks, caves, and elsewhere. In Aztec mythology, divine beings temporarily departed their space-time and infiltrated everything on earth giving them their identities, energies, and powers to live and procreate. All creatures and forces on earth and in the air were made up of subtle, eternal divine substances and hard, heavy, destructible worldly substances that served as shells to the divine substance. All life forms on earth were hard shells covering the divine substance within.

During various stages of the creation of the world some gods violated divine laws and were expelled from their cosmic region, and then came to the surface of the earth in primordial times. In one version of this creation story, a group of divinities gathered in the darkness in Teotihuacan and created a fire to help them determine the cycles of life on earth and in the heavens. One of these earthbound divinities, Nanahuatzin, threw himself in an act of self-sacrifice into the bonfire at the center of the group and descended into the underworld. As the other deities waited apprehensively around the fire in the darkness, Nanahuatzin was transformed into the first creature of the new cosmos in the form of the sun that slowly appeared above the horizon in the east. But once it appeared above the horizon, the sun stopped its upward movement and wobbled from side to side. The other gods, realizing they too had to "sacrifice" themselves in order for the first solar cycle to commence, sacrificed each other and descended into the underworld for a period of incubation. Like the sun, they acquired the heavy and destructible coverings associated with life in this space-time and appeared above the surface of the earth shrouded in these material coverings.

All the beings on the surface of the earth, such as fish and amphibians, deer and other animals of the forest, insects and birds, thus became manifestations of deities whose sacrifices and descents into the otherworld had turned them into creative beings. When these multiple sacrifices had taken place, the sun started to move on its celestial path as human, plant, and animal life began to exist. In this worldview the *self-sacrifice* of the divinities led to the creation of life in the earthly space-time. In addition, the multiple sacrifices of the gods were required to bring about the creation of the world.

Within this cyclical system of creation, destruction, and rebirth, a regular system of communication between the world of the deities and the world of creatures was established. Gods could enter and withdraw from the world through *malinalli* portals located throughout the world. The cycles of life and death, wet and dry seasons, calendars, and celestial passages were created in these ways. When a human or animal died and was buried or burned, its divine substances were released from the hard covering and returned to the underworld where it awaited the next cycle of rebirth to re-enter the world of creatures as a new, fresh being of the same type.

In the Aztec worldview, however, the gods needed nourishment, refreshment, payback, and renewal. They normally became fatigued, and in some myths they created humans who were required to worship them and make sacrificial debt-payments to them as a form of nourishment. Humans realized they were indebted to the gods for having sacrificed themselves so that life on earth could exist and be renewed, a debt that could best be paid by imitating the gods through sacrifice. Human labor and the usual offerings of fruit, meats, and ceremonial objects were important to the gods but insufficient to renew their lives. Only human blood was the truly sufficient offering to ensure the continued lives of the gods and their creative powers in the world. This resulted in an elaborate system of offerings and sacrifices designed to please, appease, and win the support of the gods with all their powers. The sun, moon, stars, and all the divine beings in the universe depended on this type of faithfulness and ritual gift-giving. The Aztecs, not having a word like "sacrifice," called the animals and humans who were ritually killed *nextlahualtin*, meaning payments or restitutions. These sacrificial entities were basically the "payback"—the prized gifts that would bring balance and renewal to the gods.

The people, plants, and animals who were sacrificed as payments were not just symbols but actually the living gods themselves. The warrior captured on the battlefield and brought into Tenochtitlan to be sacrificed was ritually transformed into a receptacle containing the divine being. When one of these image-receptacles was killed, the Aztecs repeated the creative sacrificial death the gods had undergone in the mythic times when the two space-times of the universe were first linked through sacrifice. Let us look at two examples where this sacrificial cosmovision was carried out: (1) the Great Aztec Temple itself and (2) the Feast of the Flaying of Men.

The Great Aztec Temple in splendor and blood

The various accounts of Tenochtitlan show us that the meaning and power of sacrifice is strongly linked to the *vision of place* that organized Aztec daily life. The ways they conceived of and ritually constructed the main ceremonial center of their city is the key to grasping what they believed they were up to in their monthly sacrifices of animals and humans. The Aztecs built their capital as a microcosm of the supernatural order—the material exemplar of their cosmovision, their universe on a smaller scale. This focused sense of heaven on earth was manifest in the pivot of the city and empire which was the Great Aztec Temple that each *tlatoani* took pains to enlarge or at least redecorate and renew through lavish rituals. This central temple towered above the eighty or so other ceremonial structures and became the political and ritual stage for major state spectacles that expressed a profound "cosmic security" and sense of balance that we see carved in minute detail on the massive Aztec Sun Stone.

7. Close-up of the center of the Aztec Calendar Stone depicting the four previous ages of creation and destruction around the central image of Tonatiuh, the sun deity.

However, this image of aggressive grandeur and balance also reveals that the Aztecs suffered a "cosmic paranoia," a haunting sense of insecurity, instability, and profound threats from the gods, nature, and the social landscape. The central area of the Sun Stone depicts the four previous ages of the universe in four tight boxes, each with the glyph Rain, Water, Jaguar, or Wind inside, which surround the Age of the Fifth Sun. The apparent sense of order, balance, and symmetry is challenged by the fact that each of these ages—Sun 4 Jaguar, Sun 4 Wind, Sun 4 Rain, and Sun 4 Water—is named after the force that *destroyed* the universe, and not after the force that created each cosmic period. And the Aztec age is named Sun 4 Movement in anticipation of the earthquakes prophesied to one day destroy the Aztec world, empire, and city. The myths of these repeated creations and destructions tell of periods of darkness in between the collapse of one age and the creation of a new age. This pattern of birth, fulfillment, destruction, darkness, and rebirth is the overall worldview inside which the Aztecs dwelled, constructed their capital, and lived their daily lives.

The moon goddess discovered in Mexico City

In February 1978, electrical workers excavating a pit beneath the street behind the Metropolitan Cathedral in Mexico City uncovered a massive oval stone, in mint condition, more than ten feet (3.25 m) in diameter, with the image of a contorted Aztec goddess carved on it. An anonymous phone caller informed the National Institute of Anthropology and History that a major piece of sculpture had been discovered. Archaeologists subsequently unearthed the largest monolith found anywhere in the Americas since the Sun Stone in 1790. The sensational surface image depicts a decapitated and dismembered female goddess whose precious blood is symbolized with jewels. Her striated head-cloth, stomach, arms, and legs are circled by serpents, and a skull serves as her belt buckle. She has earth-monster faces on her knees, elbows, and ankles. Her sandals indicate that she was a royal figure, and symbols on her cheek identify her as Coyolxauhqui, the sister of Huitzilopochtli.

The realization that this huge sculpture depicted the long-known myth recorded by Sahagún in the sixteenth century generated tremendous excitement among scholars of the Aztec world. This discovery caused a national thrill in Mexico and was reported

8. Coyolxauhqui Stone depicting the dismembered Goddess of the Moon.

across the globe by major news organizations. The Proyecto Templo Mayor was initiated to uncover the foundation of the entire structure of the Great Temple, which has resulted in the most expensive and most intensely excavated single structure in the Americas. One of our most important aids in understanding how the Coyolxauhqui Stone and the Great Temple represent key elements of the Aztec vision of place is a surviving *teocuicatl* (divine song), written down in the capital soon after the conquest.

The song of Huitzilopochtli

This song makes it clear that the place of Huitzilopochtli's birth and victory, called Coatepec (Serpent Mountain), is the center, axis, and symbolic "navel" of the earth. The narrative begins, "The Aztecs greatly revered Huitzilopochtli, they knew his origin, his beginning, was in this manner." The action took place on the great mountain near Tula, the ancient city associated with Quetzalcoatl, the Feathered Serpent man-god. Coatlicue (Serpent Skirt), mother of Coyolxauhqui and "the four hundred gods of the south," was sweeping out a temple when "there fell on her some plumage." She picked up the feathers, which symbolized divine semen, placed them in her blouse, and miraculously became pregnant. When her four hundred children learned of their mother's impregnation while she was working in the temple, they "were very angry, they were very agitated, as if the heart had gone out of them." The warrior daughter "Coyolxauhqui incited them, she inflamed the anger of her brothers, so that they should kill her mother." The troop of siblings prepared for war and marched a great distance to Coatepec to attack their mother. When word of the approaching attack reached the pregnant Coatlicue at Coatepec she became frightened and saddened by this threat from her children. Then her unborn son Huitzilopochtli, calmed her with the promise, "Do not be afraid, I know what I must do." Coyolxauhqui continued to inflame her siblings into a bellicose warrior troop marching toward the mountain.

At the climactic moment when Coyolxauhqui and her siblings arrived at the top of the mountain, Coatlicue gave birth to Huitzilopochtli, who miraculously appeared fully grown and dressed as a great warrior. Armed with the "serpent of fire," the most potent of Aztec swords, the patron god dismembered his sister and annihilated the other warriors, chasing them around and off the sacred hill. The text is quite specific about Coyolxauhqui's dismemberment: not only was her head cut off but her body broke into pieces as it rolled down the hill.

The excavations at the Great Temple in Mexico City reveal that this sacred myth-song was the model or vision of place used to build and rebuild Tenochtitlan's imperial shrine during the reigns of the Aztec kings. The Great Temple itself was called Coatepec and consisted of a huge pyramid supporting two temples, one dedicated to Huitzilopochtli, the other to the rain god Tlaloc. Two steep stairways led up to the shrines. The Coyolxauhqui Stone was found directly at the base of the stairway leading up to Huitzilopochtli's temple where the statue of the deity sat triumphantly at the top. On both sides of the stairway's base were two large grinning serpent heads, and numerous others jutted out elsewhere from the pyramid. The symbolic meaning of the structure is clear. The Great Temple is the architectural microcosm of Serpent Mountain. Just as Huitzilopochtli triumphed at the top of the mountain while his sister fell into pieces below, so Huitzilopochtli's shrine and icon sat triumphantly at the top of the Great Temple with the carving of the dismembered goddess found at the base of the steps. On another level, however, this sacred architecture represented the daily drama of the sun (Huitzilopochtli) rising out of the earth (Coatepec-Coatlicue) and then battling with its light the stars (the four hundred siblings) and the moon (Coyolxauhqui), which it dismembered and absorbed into its own brilliance.

This mythical drama of dismemberment was vividly repeated in numerous sacrificial rituals: for example, when enemy warriors were brought from distant battlefields (like the four hundred warriors in the myth), they were forced to climb the steps of the pyramid and undergo ritual death. In fact, we can surmise that the sacrifice of comrades witnessed by Díaz del Castillo at the Great Temple replicated this myth in which enemies who chose to attack the Hill of Coatepec met the fate of Coyolxauhqui and her siblings. The myth is emphatic about the relentless aggression of the Aztec warrior Huitzilopochtli against enemies. He drove his four hundred siblings off the mountain of the snake but did not stop there: "He pursued them, he chased them, all around the mountain ... four times—with nothing could they defend themselves. Huitzilopochtli chased them, he drove them away, he humbled them, he destroyed them, he annihilated them." In other words, the myth is a model, not for a single sacrifice but for the *escalation* of sacrifice or ritual debt payments of many individuals.

The Feast of the Flaying of Men: the city as ideal battlefield

In one of the most spectacular Aztec sacrifices, the priests and ritual choreographers turned the city into an ideal battlefield, the battlefield where nothing can go wrong for Aztec warriors. The purpose of Tlacaxipehualiztli (Feast of the Flaying of Men) was, in part, to show the youth and other citizens of the city that while the battlefield out there might be a place of victory or defeat for their armies, the ritual battlefield in here was a place of splendid, bloody victory for the Aztecs.

This transformation of the city into an ideal battlefield was accomplished over a forty-day period when captured warriors who underwent the spiritual and social change from human enemy to divine being were publicly displayed, given new names, forced to dance with their captors, and eventually sacrificed at Xipe Totec's temple or on a circular, gladiatorial stone. Their bodies were painted with long red stripes; they underwent an all-night vigil during which hair was taken from the crown of their heads, the site where their *tonalli* soul resided. This hair was guarded by the captor as a potent piece of an "eagle man" whose destiny after the sacrifice was to dwell "in the presence of the sun." Eventually, the captives, now believed to be "god-images," were seized by the hair and forced to climb the steps to the shrine of Huitzilopochtli. Some captives resisted or fainted, but some "did not act like a woman; he became strong like a man, he bore himself like a man, he went speaking like a man, he went exerting himself, he went strong of heart, he went shouting, … he went exalting his city … 'Already here I go: You will speak of me there in my home land.'" The captive was stretched out on the sacrificial stone by six priests who extracted his heart, or "precious eagle–cactus fruit," and offered its nourishing power to the sun before it was placed in the "eagle vessel." The slain captive was now called "eagle man," and like Coyolxauhqui his body was rolled "breaking to pieces, they came head over heels,...they reached the terrace at the base of the pyramid."

This fragmented body was carried by elders to the local temple where it was skinned, cut to pieces, and distributed with small pieces of flesh to be eaten by the blood relatives of the captor in a bowl of dried maize (corn) stew. The heroic captor—now decorated with bird down and chalk, and given gifts—and his cohorts wearing the sacrificial skins traveled door to door in an ancient "trick-or-treat" ritual to collect food as the new "owners of skins." According to Diego Durán, who interviewed Aztec eyewitnesses several decades later, women would bring children out to these roving "owners of skins" who took them into their arms, spoke special words, circled the courtyard of the house four times, and returned the children to their mothers, who then gave gifts to these living images of the god Xipe Totec. These movements through the neighborhoods were considered provocative displays to local males, and they often resulted in boisterous, unruly mock battles between rival groups of young Aztec warriors. These groups were watched and followed by veteran warriors dressed as Xipe Totec and Yohuallahuan (Night Drinker), who menaced and occasionally captured and ransomed them at a temple for turkey hens or mantles. These ritual movements eventually ended up at Motecuhzoma's palace with even more lavish displays as he and the rulers from Tezcoco and Tepaneca wore the skins of the most important victims and danced into the ceremonial center. There, Motecuhzoma gave an eloquent speech and distributed presents of cloaks and food to the warriors for their accomplishments.

The spectacle of Tlacaxipehualiztli culminated in a gladiatorial sacrifice, which took place in public view near the heart of the main ceremonial center. The drama of the sacrificial ritual began as great crowds entered the city. They saw the captives and their captors march in elaborate costumes, accompanied by musical outbursts, to the elevated, circular gladiatorial stone, following eagle and ocelot warriors who danced, pranced, and displayed shields and obsidian-bladed clubs raised in dedication to the sun. With sounds of conch shells, singing, and whistling, the sacrifice began when the captor seized the captive by the hair and led him to the sacrificial stone, where the captor raised a cup of the fermented beverage *pulque* four times and drank it through a long, hollow cane. The captive was made to drink *pulque* and forced onto the round stone where the "Old Bear," a priest dressed in bear skin, tied him by the ankle or waist to the center of the stone with the "sustenance rope." Given a war club decked with feathers, the captive was attacked by a dancing jaguar warrior armed with an obsidian-studded war club. If a captive somehow managed to defeat the first Aztec warrior, three others were sent in succession to destroy him. Eventually overwhelmed with slices to the calves, thighs, and chest, the captive was finished off and eventually flayed and dismembered.

The message of these ritual debt payments—"in our city, we win all battles"—was transmitted throughout Tenochtitlan. But strangers to Tenochtitlan were also present at the rituals. Foreign rulers and nobles "from cities which were his enemies from beyond the mountains,…those with which there was war, Motecuhzoma secretly summoned" to the ceremony. These princes from rival and tributary polities were guided, incognito, into a strategic, shrouded location to view the sacrifices. Placed behind arbors of flowers and branches so that they would not be seen by the citizens of Tenochtitlan, they were forced to watch as some of their finest warriors were destroyed amid cries, conch shells, trumpets, and dancing. Cosmic warfare indeed.

Chapter 5

Women and children: weavers of life and precious necklaces

Spanish chroniclers have left us a contradictory image of the lives of Aztec women. One view tells us that a woman's place was "in the heart of the home,...her home was only within the house." But when the Spaniards laid siege to the capital and the young ruler Cuauhtemoc lacked warriors to defend the city, he "had all the women ascend to the flat roofs of the houses where they made gestures of scorn to the Spaniards." Cortés "became afraid and feared that he would not be able to conquer Mexico." Women were also sacrificed in ceremonies designed to regenerate the maize fields and in one ritual a piece of a woman's thigh skin is transported to the frontier of the Aztec empire and set up on a post as a provocative dare to the male warriors of an enemy kingdom.

The primary roles of Aztec women were homemakers, priestesses, and midwives as well as rearers of children, known as "precious necklaces," in family and school. But their work, social roles, and symbolic value extended throughout the daily life of the Aztec empire even as they ruled the domesticated spaces of village and city.

Aztec women at home in the world

Many scenes in the *Codex Mendoza* portraying the Aztec lifecycle focus on the lives of females. In the bathing and naming ceremony that children underwent four days after birth, the social destiny of boys and girls was signaled by the first objects they were given to hold and play with. The male child was encouraged to touch and grab a tiny bow, arrow, and shield signaling that his destiny was that of the warrior raised to defend and strengthen the society. Girls were given miniature spinning and weaving toys and a tiny broom to prepare them for life at home where they would clean, cook, and make clothing as wives and mothers. Women were central to this ritual moment as the midwife officiated the ceremony while the recently delivered mother watched over the tub of warm water awaiting the child. These midwives were medical specialists who gave eloquent speeches to new mothers and their babies, in this case, a newborn female: "My beloved maiden, my youngest one, noblewoman, thou has suffered exhaustion, thou has become fatigued.... Our lord, the lord of the near, of the nigh, hath sent thee.... Thou wilt be in the heart of the home, thou wilt go nowhere, thou wilt nowhere become a wanderer, thou becomest the banked fire, the hearth stones."

This is an exemplary domestic scene, governed by women who were the keepers of the fire, the experts in cooking, cleaning, raising children, and maintaining the household and its center. Although largely left out of the scholarly and public story until recently, it is becoming clear just how deeply intertwined women, children, and domestic spaces were in the transmission of cultural values and all aspects of the Aztec capital, rural communities, and empire. Females were powerful domesticators of social life and their skills as cooks, weavers, designers, lovers, and healers carried their influences far beyond the family home. Recent research reveals that women gathered the sap of the maguey plants and fermented it to make the alcoholic drink *octli* (*pulque*). They raised turkeys and plants, traveled to marketplaces where they exchanged farm produce, wild herbs, salt, torches, firewood, prepared foods, and textiles. Women were valued as healers and midwives, and Sahagún emphasized that they were honored for being "strong, rugged, energetic, wiry,... exceedingly tough, animated, vigorous," while the ideal noblewoman was "patient, gentle, kind" and "worthy of being obeyed."

Women, not surprisingly, made vital contributions to the Aztec economy. They shared with males the responsibility of providing food and making clothing for the family; they were highly accomplished in transforming maize into various foods including tortillas and tamales with a myriad of sauces made from beans, tomatoes, avocados, *tomatillos*, chilies, squashes, mushrooms, waterfowl, fish, rabbits, frogs, turkeys, and dogs. Teams of mostly female cooks prepared large amounts of food for the many royal ceremonies and spectacles, and they provisioned Aztec armies during their numerous campaigns near and far from the island capital. In effect, the women fed the empire as well as the family.

Perhaps their greatest economic contribution was as weavers. Mothers and daughters carefully extracted fibers from maguey and cotton, and spun them on looms to produce widely traded textiles with attractive, intricate designs. Towns paid vast quantities of cotton in tribute to the Basin of Mexico where women turned them into capes, loincloths, skirts, and blouses, which could also be tailored to meet local demands. In a way, women wove the Aztec world together through their skills and sense of aesthetics in dressing people of all classes and ages. At the height of the empire, more than 240,000 pieces of cloth were collected yearly in tribute by the Triple Alliance and were redistributed in the central markets. Many of these pieces were elite items, which the Aztec ruler proudly awarded to government officials, noble families, warriors, and other bureaucrats in the kingdom. Women often benefited economically from these skills and contributions—some became vendors, merchants, or administrators in the marketplaces and influenced pricing practices.

The social status of women also came from their religious powers as healers and midwives. They helped maintain the health of the Aztec world and assisted every mother giving birth to the growing

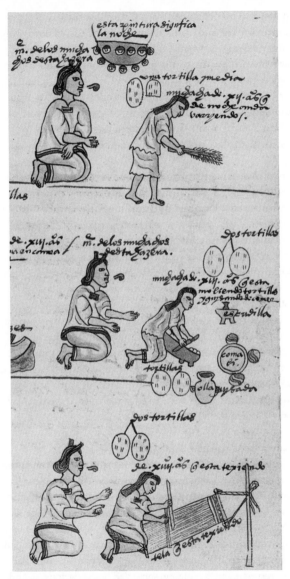

9. Aztec mothers teaching their twelve-, thirteen-, and fourteen-year-old daughters to sweep, cook, and weave.

population. This demanded that a formidable ritual, pharmacological, and mythical knowledge be passed down from mother to daughter, woman to woman. Pictorial and ethnographic sources reveal that these women mixed natural and supernatural diagnoses and treatment strategies involving animals, plants, songs, sweat baths, and storytelling. Recent studies show that Aztec women had effective knowledge of a wide range of medicinal plants, many now considered useful according to Western biomedical practices and standards.

Women also played a significant role in the priesthood. In some cases, an infant girl was taken to the temple by her mother a month or so after birth and dedicated to temple service. When she was a mature teenager, she would become a *cihuatlamacazqui* (woman priest), living a celibate life in order to focus her energies on temple duties and the yearly round of ceremonies. The festival of Ochpaniztli, dedicated to the goddess Toci (Our Grandmother), was directed by a woman priest, while an assistant called Iztaccihuatl (White Woman, because she was painted white) was responsible for decorations, preparing the ritual areas, sweeping the sacred sites, and lighting and extinguishing the ritual fires. It was possible for a woman to leave the priesthood to be married, but the suitor had to make the proper approaches to the family, the temple, and the young woman. One text tells us that a priestess could get married "if she were asked in marriage, if the words were properly said, if the fathers, the mothers, and the notables agreed."

We are fortunate to have some vivid descriptions of these priestesses dressing, dancing, and giving spirit, beauty, and power to the ceremonies. Decades after the conquest, Aztec elders recalled that "the women...were indeed carefully dressed....Some of their skirts had designs of hearts; some had a mat design like birds' gizzards; some were ornamented like coverlets; some had designs like spirals or like leaves....And some of their shifts had tawny streamers hanging, some had smoke symbols, some had dark green streamers hanging, some had house designs....And when they danced, they unbound their hair; their hair just covered each one of them like a garment. But they brought braids of their hair across their foreheads."

A special destiny awaited the souls of women who died in childbirth. These women were considered equal to warriors who died in battle or on the sacrificial stone. They too had sacrificed their own lives so that a new life could come into the world. Their souls ascended into the female side of heaven, where they dwelt together and accompanied the sun from its zenith to its setting. On certain dates their spirits would descend to earth and haunt the living to remind them of the suffering and contributions the women had made to their lives.

The sacred story and sculptures of the mother goddess Coatlicue (Serpent Skirt) and the moon goddess Coyolxauhqui (Painted Bells) demonstrate that female deities were immensely powerful in Aztec religion and daily life. Other goddesses of note included Mayahuel (*pulque*), Chalchiuhtlicue (lakes and rivers), Chicomecoatl (maize), and Huixtocihuatl (salt). These goddesses were close to the common peoples who worked as fishermen, farmers, salt gatherers, and boat people. A very popular goddess, who later became identified with the Virgin of Guadalupe, was Teteoinnan, also known as Toci, a patroness of midwives. Two fascinating goddesses were the beautiful Xochiquetzal (sexuality and feasting) and her counterpart Tlazolteotl (carnal transgression, filth, and absolution from sexual wrongdoing), who was revered by weavers, silversmiths, and sculptors.

Mothers trained their children to provide the home altars dedicated to goddesses with food, copal incense, and other acts of purification to start the day. This practice was carried on in more elaborate ways in the temple communities where priestesses tended the fires, incensed the statues of goddesses and gods, and kept them well adorned with beautifully woven and embroidered costumes.

The education of the "precious necklaces"

A father who was delivering his child to the first day of school gave this speech: "Our lord, lord of the near, of the nigh, [this child] is your property, he is your venerable child. We place him under your power, your protection with other venerable children; because you will teach him, educate him, because you will make eagles, make ocelots of them, because you instruct him for our mother, our father, Tlaltecuhtli, Tonatiuh."

These words reflect the Aztec view that education integrated humans into a wider field of being where nature, society, and the divine overlapped and interacted constantly. The reference to eagles and ocelots points toward a military vocation, and the mention of two deities shows that religious teachings were part of any Aztec curriculum. Human survival depended on the "lord of the near and nigh" who protected children and punished them with sacred powers. Aztec parents knew what all Aztec children were required to learn that their true parents were the gods.

This relationship between family, temple-schools, and the divinities was sealed during the first visit to the school when priests made incisions on the bodies of children—visible signs of social and spiritual change. The lower lips of boys were pierced and a jewel was inserted. Girls had small cuts made on their breasts and hips with obsidian blades. These incisions signified their initiation into the lifelong educational process upon which their lives depended. The Aztec equivalent of the verb "to educate" was *tlacahuapahua* or *tlacazcaltia*, which meant "to strengthen persons" or "to make persons grow." This growing and strengthening was accomplished through a series of rituals over many years that incorporated children, teenagers, and young adults into the work of the family, society, agriculture, and warfare.

Affection and discipline were the handmaidens of healthy growth in children. They were encouraged to express their feelings and attitudes openly even as they were carefully watched by their parents and given constant correction. At age four, children underwent a special growth ritual called "They Stretch Their Necks" when they were purified by fire, had their earlobes pierced and earrings inserted, and then were lifted by their foreheads and had their limbs stretched. In another ceremony held every 260 days, on the day 4 Movement, their noses, necks, ears, fingers, and legs were pulled to encourage proper growth during the next 260-day cycle. Here, the children were introduced to the sacred numbers 4 and 260 (associated with the four directions of the cosmos and the completion of the ritual calendar), which would continue to guide them even after death. Some Spanish priests remarked on the high quality of Aztec childcare and recorded numerous eloquent praises spoken to children by their parents and midwives. For instance, young girls were called "my precious necklace, thou who art my precious feather,...my creation,...my blood, my color, my image."

Young Aztecs were given meticulous instructions on personal hygiene, social graces, and what to avoid in their daily lives. Eight teachings were given to the children of well-to-do families. The first involved spending some nights in pious vigil praying to the "lord of the near and nigh" during which they would offer incense and sweep the temple or home. The second admonished them to walk in public with upright postures, prudence, and dispatch "lest thou be named fool, shameless." Children were not to look directly into anyone's eyes when speaking, especially when talking to people outside the family. Staring at a woman, especially a married woman, was considered a clear sexual advance and could be severely punished. Gossip and rumor-mongering was to be avoided at all costs for in the Aztec world, plots of a social or magical nature inevitably led to a life of crime. Showing up for work or appointments on time was crucial as the Aztecs loathed laziness, negligence, and haughtiness. Priests sometimes hit lazy persons with a club. A public dress code emphasized neatness and the avoidance of ostentatious display. Capes were to be carefully tied to cover the shoulder or else the person would be thought a buffoon, a mad person, and graceless. Public speaking was to be done softly with proper rhythm and breath control. Sounding like a groaning or squeaking person was to be strictly avoided. Finally, the strongest warnings concerned what one put into one's mouth. Prudent eating and drinking was a virtue; gluttony and sloppiness was considered physically and socially reprehensible and dangerous. Hands and faces had to be washed before each meal and when eating with others. "Do not quickly seat thyself… and when the eating is over, thou art quickly to seize the washbowls" went the instruction.

Scenes from the *Codex Mendoza* show that strict discipline included punishments for unacceptable behaviors, including laziness, rudeness, and boastfulness. Seriously disobedient boys had their hands and feet bound and maguey thorns stuck into their shoulders, backs, and buttocks. When reprimands failed to change behavior, the disobedient were forced to inhale chili smoke or were tied hand and foot and made to sleep on damp ground all night. The Aztecs had a saying they applied to unruly children indicating the seriousness of bad behavior. It went "*Anjtlanammati, Anjtlatamati,*" meaning "I heed no mother, I heed no father."

The source of these harsh measures was, in part, the Aztec perception that they dwelled within a hazardous cosmos full of social and spiritual dangers and eruptions of chaos in the forms of diseases, wild animals, earthquakes, storms, rivals, and enemies. "On earth we travel, we live along a mountain peak. Over here there is an abyss, over there is an abyss. Wherever thou art to deviate, wherever thou art to go astray, there wilt thou fall, there wilt thou plunge into the deep."

The Aztecs constantly preached discipline and frugality, especially in relation to sexual promiscuity and drunkenness. Sexual activity before marriage was considered dangerous because it led to skin ailments and death. Both males and females were pressured to abstain from sex until married as it protected the heart from being infected with "excrement" and self destruction. The young woman was a "precious green stone, yet a precious turquoise," who was to be kept clean, pure, and without sexual experience until a husband was chosen. Young women were also taught that when the right young man came along, the one sent by one of the divinities (meaning a match made in heaven), the young woman must be ready to commit herself all the way. "Give thyself not to the wanderer, to the restless one who is given to pleasure, to the evil youth...When thou hast seen the one who, together with thee he will endure to the end, do not abandon him. Seize him, hang onto him even though he be a poor person, even though he be a poor eagle warrior, a poor ocelot warrior."

Young Aztec males also felt these pressures pushing hard against the desires of puberty. In order to achieve a "good heart" the young man should emulate devout priests, penitents, chaste men, elders, scribes, and warriors who brought honor to themselves in war, and avoid "lust for vice, for filth...that which is deadly. For the lord of the near, of the nigh, hath said, thou art ordained one woman for one man,...thou art not to devour, to gulp down the carnal life as if thou wert a dog." The real goal was sexual control so as to produce in marriage rugged, agile children who were clean and beautiful. We can appreciate these intense messages when we learn that for the Aztecs, a sexual transgression injured not just the person committing the immoral act but the parents, siblings, and friends of the trespasser as well. Sexual misconduct grew into a social contagion, a spiritual-psychological virus, a noxious force that grew and spread through the family, neighborhood, and friends.

Education in the *calmecac* included military, mechanical, astrological, and religious training. Youths, both male and female (but in separate schools), were taught from large pictorial manuscripts telling of the genealogy, history, geography, mythology, laws, and arts of society. As in other schools, songs and dances were central to *calmecac* life. Divine songs telling of the lives of gods, dreams, and the calendar were taught, recited, danced, and sung. Although this school was particularly attractive to noble families, it appears that common folk also dedicated their children to the rigors and riches of the *calmecac*.

Another important school was the *telpochcalli*, or "young man's house," where the great majority of fifteen-year-old boys, mostly commoners, were trained for military life. Since the *telpochcalli* involved focused preparation for warfare, the school's instructors demanded from these youths total attention, great physical effort, bravery, and the ability to withstand intense pain. The entire society believed that its well-being depended on the training and courage of its defenders, and it put major demands on the *telpochcalli* to develop powerful warriors.

A hard lesson for Aztec youth

While Aztecs greatly enjoyed pleasure, skillful wordplay, and many types of art, they also learned the harder lessons about human life. Even today in some indigenous communities the following song is sung:

> We live here on this earth
> We are all fruits of the earth
> The earth sustains us
> We grow here, on the earth and flower
> And when we die
> We wither in the earth
> We are all fruits of the earth
> We eat of the earth
> Then the earth eats us.

A vision of reciprocity between humans, nature, and the gods was taught early to Aztec children who heard that the earth was not only a garden that fed us but also a hungry mouth: cosmic jaws that demanded to be fed by humans. All humans would suffer death, which was a destruction and fragmentation, but it was also an entrance into another world where another kind of life existed, regulated by rituals. Children were also reassured that if they died in early childhood they would have a good afterlife and be suckled by a tree in paradise. When young children died they became green stones and precious turquoise and bracelets. They did not go to the terrible place of icy winds called Mictlan but rather to Xochatlalpan (Place of the Abundance of the Water of Flowers), where they suckled from an eternal tree of sustenance.

As one grew older, however, the options for life and life after death grew more diverse. Children learned how their bodies contained not one but three animistic entities whose ultimate destinies were determined by the manner in which one lived and died. These three "souls" were the *tonalli*, located in the head, which was the soul of will and intelligence; the *teyolia*, located in the heart, which was the soul of fondness and vitality; and the *ihiyotl*, located in the liver, which was the soul of passion, luminous gas, and aggression. All three were gifts from the gods deposited in the human body, but animals, plants, and objects also had animistic forces within them. At the time of death, these three souls dispersed into different regions of the universe. Although the texts about this separation of souls are not always consistent, it appears that they could go to one of four places: Mictlan, in the underworld, for those who died an ordinary death; the sun in the sky, for warriors who died in combat, people sacrificed to the sun, and women who died while giving birth for the first time; Tlalocan, the rain god's mountain paradise, for those whose death was caused by water or water-related forces like frost or cold sicknesses; or Chichihualcuauhco, which was exclusively reserved for infants who died while still nursing from their mothers, that is, who had not yet eaten from the earth.

One interesting teaching was that a divine dog, which dwelled in the afterlife, could assist in the journey of the *teyolia* soul. The flames of cremation would beckon the dog in the underworld at the shore of a subterranean river to help the soul of the dead cross to the other side, where gift offerings were made to Mictlantecuhtli, the Lord of the Dead. Sacrificed warriors were believed to carry the gifts of war they had worn or held when they were dispatched on the sacrificial stone. In some cases these included the feathers of powerful birds that would help them, in the afterlife, to fly across the heavens with the sun.

It appears that at least one of the souls, the *teyolia*, which resided in the heart, did not leave the body until cremation. This was especially true of a dead ruler, who could still be in communication, through the *teyolia*, with his ministers until his body was burned. The fire that consumed the cadaver carried the soul on its journey to its appropriate place in the afterlife. The fire ritual was the occasion when relatives made offerings, shed tears, and said prayers at the hearth. These ritual actions protected the soul and gave it strength during its dangerous journey. In the case of certain rulers, the servants were sacrificed and cremated on a nearby pyre, but their hearts were extracted and burned on the same pyre as the dead *tlatoani*. These hearts, the *teyolia* of the servants, along with vessels of invigorating drinks and royal clothes, accompanied the soul of the ruler and protected it on its journey.

This means that the Aztecs had a practice somewhat similar to the cult of relics we associate with medieval Europe. The bones of rulers and others who attained a divine reputation while alive were kept in special containers (boxes, vases, or jars) and displayed or buried in temples. They would receive offerings and, in exchange, the souls of the deceased would lend strength and protection to the community. A number of these relic containers have been excavated at the Great Aztec Temple in the last thirty years.

A powerful religious imagination was imparted to growing children during their schooling in the *calmecac* or *telpochcalli*. They learned that the souls of the dead could travel to an afterlife, but parts could also stay close to the family, city, or community because they were not confined to the physical limits of the body or its remains. One could be inspired, enhanced, or haunted by these lingering parts of souls. The souls of the dead could also become attached to and integrated within gods or goddesses, thus revitalizing them. This was particularly true of rulers, great warriors, and distinguished artists and poets. The one outstanding example was Topiltzin Quetzalcoatl, who ruled the fabled Toltecs. It is said that when he was cremated, his *teyolia* rose up into the sky and changed into the planet Venus, which the Toltecs called Tlahuizcalpantecuhtli, the Lord of the House of Dawn.

Beings of all kinds—plants, gods, animals, humans, insects, water, and stones—shared in a co-essence, and the closeness of humans and gods was evident in the burial practices. The Spanish friar Bartolomé de las Casas, who spent years living among, ministering to, and protecting indigenous peoples, witnessed and participated in many burials. He wrote about the elaborate speeches, rites, and mourning practices, and reported that people commonly dressed the deceased in the different clothes and insignia of the gods. Children were clothed as the god they believed to be their protector; merchants were dressed as merchant gods; the families of those individuals executed for adultery made small images of Tlazolteotl, the goddess of sexual transgression. For those who drowned, their families made images of the water god, Tlaloc, in hopes he would watch after their souls in the afterlife.

Chapter 6
Wordplay, philosophy, sculpture

The Aztec world presents us with a profound paradox. How could a society so committed to cosmic regeneration through the expansion of warfare and the thrust of the ceremonial knife be so skilled and accomplished in featherwork, poetry, sculpture, and childrearing? How could a people who spent so much energy, organization, blood, and wealth in efforts to obtain and sacrifice humans and animals conceive and carve the marvelous Sun Stone, design and execute scores of other masterpieces, and organize one of the greatest architectural landscapes in urban history? Although nearly everyone has heard something about the Aztecs' bloodletting rites, almost no one knows they were renowned wordsmiths and riddlers whose philosophic formulations greatly impressed many Spaniards. Yet the Aztec image that stares at us through the ensemble of evidence is one of startling juxtaposition of flowers, songs, and blood.

Nowhere is this paradox more clearly presented than in the aesthetic creations of Aztec *tlacuiloque* (scribes), sculptors, and *tlamatinime* (teacher-philosophers). Aztec memory traced their superb aesthetic practices back to the Toltec kingdom of Quetzalcoatl, where they believed wisdom, calendars, featherwork, sculpture, and turquoise and green stone jewelry was perfected. This lineage back to the creative era of the Feathered Serpent reveals the understanding that artwork, like everything else, was infused with divine forces that originated beyond human genius but chose humans as the conduit for regenerative powers expressed in art, architecture, theater, and agriculture. The cultural paragon for Aztec art and social space was the city of Tollan, as Sahagún recorded that the "Toltec house...consisted of four abodes. One was facing east; this was the house of gold; that which served as the stucco was gold plate joined to it. One was facing west, toward the setting sun; this was the house of green stone, the house of fine turquoise.... One was facing south, toward the irrigated lands, this was the house of shells or of silver.... One was facing north, toward the plains,... this was the red house; red because red shells were inlaid in the interior walls."

This commitment to a balanced order of city and cosmos continued up into Aztec times, and it was beautifully elaborated in many arts and crafts including goldworking, featherworking, poetry, and human speech as well as sculpture. But let us begin with the fun found in some Aztec riddles and proverbs.

Wordplay and riddles

It may come as a surprise that the Aztecs were great riddlers. Their superb use of words went beyond the eloquent, balanced, rhythmic oratory of rulers, priests, and midwives to include the wordplay of aphorisms, metaphors, and riddles. The surviving literature reveals that these linguistic puzzles added imagery and levity to conversations on nearly any topic. For instance, this one referring to clouds and the atmospheric realm: "What is a little blue-green jar filled with popcorn? Someone is sure to guess our riddle: it is the sky." The underworld is played upon in the simple act of gathering water: "What is a little water jar to carry upon the head, which knows the land of the dead? One can see from our little riddle that it is the pottery pitcher for drawing water." And a metaphor for the common cold: "What is that which is a hill whence there is a flow? Our nose." Moving to the insect world we find: "What is it that goes along the foothills of the mountain patting our tortillas with its hands? A butterfly." And warning the walker to be alert: "What is a tiny colored stone sitting on the road? Dog excrement." And this short yet ample homage to the most sacred plant of all: "What is it that bends over us all over the world? The maize tassel."

The Aztecs also enjoyed using proverbs to educate, inspire, and describe the human condition. Consider this expression of parental pride for a productive child: "*Ipal nonixpatlaoa*: because of him my face becomes wide. This was said when someone's child—a boy or girl—or else someone's pupil, was well-taught, well-brought up." And referring to a life of fame and public significance, in Aztec times and even after the Spaniards arrived: "*Mixtitlan, aiauhtitlan*: in the clouds, in the mist. This was said of the highly esteemed, the very great; of those never before seen, of those never before known, nor anywhere seen in times of yore. So here in all Mexico it was thus said that the Spaniards came emerging from within the clouds, within the mist." And this paradoxical appreciation: "*Yollotl, eztli*: heart and blood. These words were said of chocolate because in the past it was precious and rare. The common people and the poor did not drink it. They also said it was deranging and it was thought to be like the mushroom, for it intoxicated people." The practice of ritual death by sacrificial knife had its own saying: "*In ie tlecujlixquac, in ie tlamamatlac*: already at the edge of the fire, already at the stairway. This was said of those who were about to be put to death, who already had been brought up to die; or they had already been placed at the edge of the fire; it was time for them to die."

Scribes and moral philosophy

When Bernardino de Sahagún began his evangelical work and linguistic research among the Aztecs, he became deeply impressed with their profound rhetorical practices. The first manuscript he produced in 1547 contained more than forty *huehuetlatolli*, ancient discourses recovered from interviews with native elders. When this material appeared in Book 6 of the *Florentine Codex*, he called it "Rhetoric and Moral Philosophy" because of the florid, highly formal use of parallelism, metaphors, and careful repetitions in prayers, public speeches, and proclamations. These rhetorical formulas were effective instruments for organizing human behavior through a moral imperative. They often involved *difrasismos* or metaphoric couplets that combined to signify a third meaning. Their speeches were filled with dual symbolism and were spoken on many occasions, including the coronation of a ruler, the entry of a youth into the *calmecac*, the work of a midwife, or a wedding.

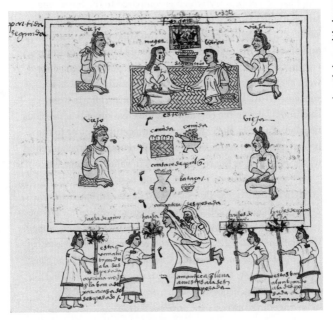

10. Wedding scene. A knot links the newlyweds sitting on the woven mat as their parents offer advice as indicated by speech glyphs.

Consider this speech given by a midwife to a newly delivered mother and notice how elements of Aztec cosmovision infiltrate the speech and guide its main point:

> My beloved maiden, brave woman, thou hast worked like a slave, thou hast labored, thou hast become an eagle warrior, thou hast become as an ocelot warrior: thou hast raised up, thou hast taken to the shield, the small shield. Thou hast exerted thyself, thou hast encountered, imitated our mother Cihuacoatl, Quilaztli. Now our lord hath placed thee upon the eagle warrior reed mat, upon the ocelot warrior reed mat. Thou has returned exhausted from battle, my beloved maiden, brave woman; be welcome.

This welcoming speech—to a wife transformed into a mother—emphasizes her bravery, which is compared to the life-giving labors of the mother goddesses Cihuacoatl-Quilaztli and the successful battlefield efforts of the two great warrior types (eagle and ocelot) in the Aztec armies. Repeated hundreds of times a year in the Aztec communities, the speech shows us that words were art forms, and childbirth was profoundly valued as a supreme creative act. These artistic and brave efforts were celebrated later in the ceremony as the creation of the "precious necklaces," that is, the children who are gathered close to the bosom, shoulder, and neck by caring parents, the precious child who is also seen as the continuation of a valued lineage:

> Here the truth is that through our lord we … see in our dreams,… the face of one who hath arrived, the precious necklace, the precious feather, the baby, that which here hath been flaked off. Here in the humble mound of dirt, in the humble reed enclosure the master, our lord the creator, the master, Quetzalcoatl, flaketh off a precious necklace, placeth a precious feather. Here on your neck, in your bosoms, in your hands he placeth … the incomparable, the wonderful, the precious, the priceless, the rare.

Huehuetlatlolli were cultivated and taught by philosopher-priests called *tlamatinime* ("knowers of things"), who were renowned as the living embodiments of wisdom and the artistic pathways to achieving it:

> The wise man: a light, a torch, a stout torch that does not smoke....
> His are the black and red ink, his are the illustrated manuscripts, he
> studies the illustrated manuscripts. He himself is writing and wisdom.
> He is the path, the true way for others. He puts a mirror before others;
> he makes them prudent, cautious; he causes a face to appear in them.

These philosopher-teachers were exemplars of clarity and the pathway to truth on earth. They were the wise men who would not throw smoke in the eyes of people but could reveal to the student their true nature or face. The reference to the "black and red ink" means that *tlamantinime* were the keepers of the books that contained the history, genealogy, and theology of the culture. The true teacher, then, was an artist whose abilities could *delve into the face of other humans*, helping them achieve an identity, an understanding of who they were in this Aztec world of precious impermanence. One poem by the great priest-king Nezahualcoyotl (Hungry Coyote) says it best:

> I comprehend the secret, the hidden:
> O my lords! Thus we are, we are mortal, men through and through,
> we all will have to go away, we all will have to die on earth.
> Like a painting, we will be erased.
> Like a flower we will dry up here on earth...
> Think on this my lords, eagles, and ocelots, though you be of jade,
>   though you be of gold, you will also go there, to the place of
>   the fleshless.

This is the cosmic condition illuminated by the stout torch, which shows that human life is unstable and illusory. How then

Wordplay, philosophy, sculpture

does one know the truth or reality that exists beyond this world, that is, not just the "place of the fleshless" or the death of Mictlan in the underworld? The answers were given, in part, through art, especially the art of poetic words and language such as the *huehuetlatolli*. The *tlamatinime* developed a rhetorical strategy aimed at discovering and experiencing the nature of truth, a solid foundation in the world. They believed that there was such a reality beyond human existence, "in the region of the gods above and in the region of the dead below." To penetrate these regions and discover a stable reality, they had to devise techniques to open the depths of the human personality to the profound world of truth. The main technique was the creation of *in xochitl, in cuicatl* (flowers and songs)—artistic expression in the forms of words, songs, and paintings that connected the human personality ("face and heart") with the divine. The divine or true foundation of the cosmos was understood in terms of a duality that pervaded all levels and regions of the world. In Aztec culture, a supreme dual god, Ometeotl, originally created the cosmos. This duality was manifested in combinations such as male/female, hot/cold, left/right, underworld/celestial world, above/below, darkness/light, rain/drought, and life/death. For the Aztecs, the best instruments for expressing a human duality that reflected and communicated the dual dimensions of the divinity were metaphors that generally consisted of two words or phrases joined to form a single idea, like "flower and song," meaning poetry or truth. In other words, the divine duality of Ometecuhtli and Omecihuatl that together made Ometeotl, the Giver of Life, was a *difrasismo*, or two things that together meant something else. Other popular *difrasismos* included the following:

in atl, in tepetl: water and hill: a town
in topan, in mictlan: what is above us and the region of the dead: the world beyond humans
topco, petlacalco: in the bag and in the box: a secret
in cueitl, in huipilli: the skirt, the blouse: the sexual nature of women

In order for this knowledge and methods of attaining it to be communicated effectively, the work of the *tlacuilo* was crucial. These artists working closely with the *tlamatinime* were the makers of the screenfold codices and mural paintings. Again, these teachers and artists were modeled after the divine scribe, Ometeotl, the Dual God.

> With flowers You write,
> O Giver of Life;
> With songs You give color,
> With songs You shade
> those who live here on the earth.
> Later You will erase eagles and tigers,
> We live only in Your book of paintings,
> here, on the earth.

This poem depicts Ometeotl, the Dual God, as a writer, a singer, and a painter. The Giver of Life is the divine artist who sings and *paints human life into existence in his/her divine book*. The message is also that "those who live here on the earth" are perishable, existing for only a short time. The world is created by the "flowers and songs" of the gods. If gods painted the world in a book, then the human painter, the *tlacuilo*, "he who paints in the red and black ink," was the artist closest to the gods.

A recent "rediscovery" of an indigenous pictorial map reveals just how much cultural information, teaching, cosmology, and religious practices were encoded in the products of the "red and black" painters. The *Mapa de Cuauhtinchan No. 2* is a beautiful 3×6-foot painted manuscript from the 1540s, brought into public light by the Mexican philanthropist Ángeles Espinosa Yglesias. It has more than seven hundred images depicting the worldview, pilgrimages, encounters with different ethnic groups, meeting with deities, and ethnobotany of peoples who, though older than the Aztec culture of Tenochtitlan, were eventually integrated into the Aztec empire. The surviving map is actually *stories in pictures*, that is, a large collection of place names, processions, natural catastrophes, cultural discoveries, myths, and events that cover more than three hundred years of pre-Hispanic history and a territory stretching over several modern-day states in Mexico. If these journeys, symbols, practices, and memories were written out in European script, the resulting epic could well be compared to the grand narratives of the *Iliad* and the *Odyssey*. It tells of the long and arduous journeys of the Chichimecs who emerge from the Place of Seven Caves at the pleading of two Toltec priests (Feather Lip and Serpent Foot) from the great pilgrimage city of Cholula. Writing with pictures was not only a way of transmitting information and knowledge but also, as mentioned earlier, the way of bringing "heart," the deepest truths of the community and therefore God and the gods into the viewers' and listeners' minds. This is the power of the painter of stories and the codices, maps, and other paintings of sacred knowledge.

Sculpture: living stones

When the Spaniards made their march from the coast of Yucatan to the Basin of Mexico they were surprised that the great number and diversity of religious images decorating homes, towns, temples, walkways, caves and heights of mountains, and crossroads surpassed the sophisticated culture of religious imagery in Spain. Maya, Tlaxcalan, and Aztec peoples were seeking contact with divine powers everywhere in the forms of wooden, earthen, stone, and vegetal images of gods, royal families, powerful animals, the sun, moon, and stars, crabs and butterflies, and even fleas. Unfortunately this superb collection of sculptures in various media was the target of Spain's destructive religious campaign against "idols" and "idolatry"—terms that were used to justify the annihilation of indigenous people and their artistic achievements in New Spain. A surprising number of world class sculptures survive because they were either buried by natives themselves during the various reconstructions of their temples or utilized as fill or support in the foundations of the plazas, churches, and civic buildings they constructed in the colonial period.

Both the ubiquity of these creations and the intensity of the Spanish attacks on them point to their special powers in the Aztec imagination. These objects were venerated because they were considered living, divine beings. Each sculpture, often adorned with clothing and flowers, was understood as an *ixiptla* or god image that was like a skin or shell of a numinous being.

A sign that magical forces were believed to dwell in these sculptures was the Aztec practice of snatching stone and wooden images from conquered peoples' temples and territories and carrying them back, in jubilation, and depositing them in a temple in the center of Tenochtitlan. These captured sculptures signaled not only the defeat of the town they represented but also the Aztec acquisition of the cosmo-magical powers embedded in the statues. As the Aztecs expanded their imperial lands, increased the size of their buildings, and rebuilt the Great Aztec Temple, they also cultivated a superb, virile, artistic program that was most forcefully manifested in the hundreds of monuments depicting gods, warriors, rulers, and cosmic forces.

Chapter 7
The fall of the Aztec empire

How could the Aztec empire, with its powerful military tradition, complex religious institutions, and long-range trading and spy system, fall to a conflicted group of Spanish invaders in less than two years and on home ground? In this fragment of a pre-conquest song, the Aztecs expressed supreme confidence in their city and worldview:

> Proud of itself
> Is the city of Mexico-Tenochtitlan.
> Here no one fears to die in war.
> This is our glory.
> This is Your Command,
> O Giver of Life!
> Have this in mind, O princes,
> Do not forget it.
> Who could conquer Tenochtitlan?
> Who could shake the foundation of the heavens?

Between Easter Sunday 1519 and August 13, 1521, the Aztec capital and its complex social pyramid were broken at the top and profoundly transformed throughout. In a Spanish triumphal view constructed by Bernal Díaz del Castillo, Hernán Cortés, and generations of subsequent writers, the extraordinary courage and ingenuity of five hundred Spanish soldiers brought

Tenochtitlan to its knees—a testament to Iberian cultural superiority. Yet many aspects of this "conquest" have seldom been adequately understood. Although the Spaniards had superior military technology (cannons, harquebuses, and crossbows), their success was more the result of the massive indigenous armies that fought the Aztecs with Cortés and the rapid spread of European diseases that devastated the native population, including the royal family. Another factor was the effective translations by one of the most fascinating female figures in history, Malintzin, alternatively known as doña Marina or La Malinche. Also worth mentioning was the identification of Cortés with the returning man-god Quetzalcoatl. The so-called conquest was as much an indigenous civil war and rebellion by the Aztecs' enemies, who formed crucial alliances with the Spaniards and supplied thousands of native warriors who served under Cortés's leadership.

When Cortés and his men arrived in Cozumel in 1519, one of the first words they recognized spoken by the natives was "Castilan" (Castilian). It turned out that two shipwrecked Spaniards had been living on the mainland since 1511. Searching inland, Cortés found one, a Spanish priest named Gerónimo de Aguilar, who lived as a laborer in a Maya community and spoke their language but retained his native Spanish. Aguilar told Cortés of another survivor, Gonzalo Guerrero, who had become a Maya war chief in another town. While Aguilar was happy to be rescued, Guerrero had married an Indian woman, had children with her, gotten tattooed in the native style, and become a war captain. In the social and military drama that followed, Aguilar aided the Spaniards by translating crucial information for them as they attempted to form alliances with indigenous communities, some of which harbored deep antipathy for the Aztecs. Guerrero stayed on the Maya side and helped them resist and fight the Spaniards at all costs. His tattooed body apparently was found among the Maya killed in a fight with the Spaniards, south of Yucatan, in 1535.

The three tongues

The subsequent defeat of the Aztec nobles, warriors, and Motecuhzoma was accomplished by many forces, not least the power of language. Communication between these two peoples was extremely confusing, and misunderstanding was the rule in the early meetings, in part because three languages, not two, were involved. The key person serving as a language bridge was neither Aguilar nor Cortés but Malintzin, whom the Spaniards called doña Marina. She spoke both a Mayan dialect and the Nahuatl of the Aztecs, and eventually learned basic Spanish. After the Spaniards won a battle against a Maya community, she and a few other women were given to Cortés. She became one of his mistresses and bore him his favorite son, Martín. She accompanied the Spaniards during their march to the central plateau and played a crucial role during the meetings between Cortés and Motecuhzoma. Díaz del Castillo gave her tremendous credit for Spanish victories: "This was the great beginning of our conquests and thus, thanks be to God, things prospered with us…because without the help of doña Marina we could not have understood the language of New Spain and Mexico." She appears in a number of paintings by native and colonial artists in the act of translating at key meetings between Spaniards and native lords. Today in Mexico she is known as La Malinche and has been the subject of not only derisive books about her as a traitor to native Mesoamericans but also admiring books about her intelligent and shrewd tactics of bridging the cultures that constitute Mexico.

The hazardous road to the Great City of Mexico

Early in their explorations and battles with coastal Maya peoples, news came that somewhere in the distance stood a great and wealthy kingdom in the highlands. Each time the invaders pressed local chiefs for more gold and trade goods, they were pointed in that direction, and Cortés became obsessed with finding his way to what he called the "Great City of Mexico." Along the way, the

11. **Doña Marina serving as interpreter between Aztec nobles and Spaniards, redrawn from the *Florentine Codex*.**

Spaniards discerned that there were many city-states whose intense political and economic rivalries could be played against one another, which Cortés accomplished with remarkable skill. Meanwhile, Motecuhzoma repeatedly sent nobles acting as his spies to meet the Spaniards and discern their military strength, and through the work of Aztec artists, provide images of their ships, weapons, armor, dogs, and horses. Cortés soon founded a settlement, Villa Rica de la Vera Cruz (Rich Town of the True Cross) and in a shrewd political maneuver had himself designated its legal representative, thereby bypassing his patron and superior Governor Velásquez in Cuba and establishing his authority in New Spain directly under the king. Cortés quickly managed a crucial alliance with the Totonacs of Cempoala who revealed that they wanted out from under Aztec dominance. The Totonacs provided warriors and porters, and thus strengthened Spanish maneuverability with cannons and supplies. This alliance was the first of many, and the troop heading for Tenochtitlan burgeoned into a multiethnic army.

The critical turning point in Spanish military fortunes took place when Cortés led this army to the outskirts of Tlaxcala, a large, prosperous confederacy made up of four provinces. The Tlaxcalans had successfully resisted Aztec domination for many years even though they were surrounded by provinces allied with Motecuhzoma. When the Tlaxcalans refused Cortés's entreaties to form an alliance, the Spaniards launched a series of attacks against them; they counterattacked and began to weaken the Spanish advantage. After serious casualties on both sides, the two entered into an alliance against the Aztecs, which proved absolutely crucial to Spanish success in the months ahead.

Soon, this multiethnic army headed for Tenochtitlan by way of Cholula, the great pilgrimage center of central Mesoamerica, which had recently become allied with Motecuhzoma. While feigning a desire for political alliance, Cortés had his soldiers surround and massacre a huge group of Cholula's population, including women and children, assembled in the main courtyard. With their powerful military reputation proceeding them, the Spanish, Tlaxcalan, and Cempoalan warriors crossed the mountains between Iztaccihuatl and Popocatepetl and descended into the southern lake region of the Basin of Mexico. As Motecuhzoma waited, Cortés led a sizable contingent up the causeway from Iztapalapa into the capital where greetings, gift exchanges, and the grand tour (see chap. 1) took place. Motecuhzoma housed them in spacious palaces and enticed them with sumptuous gifts of gold, silver, and women. But after several weeks the Spaniards, alerted by rumors of rebellions, attacks, and betrayals, eventually took Motecuhzoma prisoner in his own palace where he became a puppet ruler.

Spanish massacres and the murder of Motecuhzoma

Before long, news from the coast reached Cortés that the Spanish governor in Cuba had sent another Spanish contingent to arrest him for violating the contract terms of his expedition. Nineteen ships filled with 1,400 men armed with twenty cannons and scores of horseman and crossbowmen arrived and presented Cortés with the greatest political challenge of his career. He confronted this rival force with a surprise attack and persuasive stories of victories, heroism, wealth, and women. He successfully convinced the majority of the soldiers to abandon their original purpose and thus gained an army of Spaniards now three times the size of what he had arrived with months before. Just as this triumph was accomplished, terrible news arrived from the capital. Cortés had left his most able and brutal lieutenant Pedro de Alvarado in charge of Motecuhzoma, the palace, and the city. Díaz del Castillo left this poignant description of what transpired:

> Let me say how ill luck suddenly turned the wheel and after great good fortune and pleasure follows sadness,... it so happened that at this moment came the news that Mexico was in revolt and that Pedro de Alvarado was besieged in his fortress and quarters,... there arrived four great chieftains sent to Cortés by the great Motecuhzoma to complain to him... with tears streaming from their eyes, that Pedro de Alvarado sallied out from his quarters with all the soldiers and for no reason at all, fell on their Chieftains and Caciques who were dancing and celebrating in honor of their idols and he killed and wounded many of them.

The massacre of hundreds of unarmed Aztec nobles and musicians during a yearly ceremony dedicated to the god Tezcatlipoca has become a moment of infamy in Mexican memory as an act of extreme Spanish cruelty. According to several indigenous accounts, the finest Aztec warriors gathered to sing and dance "with all their hearts so that Spaniards would marvel at the beauty of the rituals" but "at that moment in the feast, when the dance was loveliest and when song was linked to song, the Spaniards were seized with an urge to kill the celebrants." The Spaniards blocked the exits of the ceremonial precinct and brutally attacked the dancers and musicians, beheading drummers, disemboweling men and women, "their entrails hanging out, . . . arms were torn from bodies, some attempted to run away but their intestines dragged as they ran, . . . they seemed to tangle their feet in their own entrails." Terrified, some celebrants tried to hide by pretending to lie dead among the victims. Following the slaughter, weeping mothers and fathers of the dead came to look for bodies, which they collected and ceremonially burned at a sacred shrine called the Eagle Urn.

Aztec hospitality and political confusion was replaced by all-out revolt against the Spaniards. By the time Cortés returned with his troops on June 24, 1520, the Aztecs had turned the city into a trap, and mayhem ensued. The Aztecs assaulted the enlarged Spanish and Tlaxcalan forces for twenty-three straight days, killing them in their quarters and when they came out to fight. Aztec assassins picked off stray Spaniards and even those Mexica suspected of helping them. When the Aztecs repulsed Cortés's attempt to negotiate his withdrawal from the city, he forced Motecuhzoma out onto a roof to plead for peace. The *tlatoani* was murdered— some say strangled by the Spaniards for fear he would incite a greater revolt, others say stoned to death by his own subjects for his poor leadership. The murdered ruler's brother, Cuitlahuac, who had earlier urged resistance against the Spaniards, led a massive attack and, on a rainy night, drove the Spaniards out of the city. In what is known today as the Noche Triste (Night of Sadness) and in the desperate days of retreat that followed, more than eight hundred Spaniards (including five women) and two thousand Tlaxcalan warriors were killed. During the Noche Triste it is reported that Spanish and Tlaxcalan bodies filled the canals to such a depth that survivors walked across the water on top of them. Some four hundred Spaniards, all of them wounded, barely

escaped the city and, humiliated in defeat, dragged themselves out
of the Basin of Mexico and back to the allied area of Tlaxcala,
fighting rear guard actions most of the way. Once in Tlaxcala, they
recuperated for five and a half months and worked closely with
the Tlaxcalan nobles and military units to plan Spanish vengeance
in the form of a siege and invasion of Tenochtitlan.

The siege and fall of Tenochtitlan

European microbes also came to Cortés's aid and proved to be
some of the most effective warriors of all. During this five-month
period, an epidemic of smallpox swept through the Aztec
population, killing warriors, nobles, and commoners. Cuitlahuac,
the new ruler who had led the assault on Cortés, died two months
later. As astonishing as it seems, within a year, 40 percent of the
indigenous population of Central Mexico had died of smallpox.
The Aztecs later recalled their misery: "There was hunger. Many
died of famine. There was no more good, pure water to drink—
only nitrous water. Many died of it—contracted dysentery, which
killed them. The people ate anything—lizards ..."

To ensure the success of the upcoming siege, Cortés made two
decisive military decisions. First, he ordered the construction of
thirteen brigantines by Spanish and Tlaxcalan carpenters back in
Tlaxcala, out of sight of Aztec spies. The Spaniards recovered sails,
anchors, and rigging from the ships they had scuttled on the coast,
and this equipment along with arms, gunpowder, harquebuses,
and crossbows was carried back to Tlaxcala. Eventually these
small ships, forty-two feet long, built in sections, were transported
over the mountains and down to the city of Tezcoco where they
were assembled. For several months, Cortés led a contingent of
Spanish and Tlaxcalan warriors to circumambulate the lake
region, spy on Aztec defenses, weaken Aztec allies, and build
alliances with Aztec enemies who played crucial roles in the
upcoming battle. When the attack and siege of the city was
launched in May 1521, the Spaniards numbered 700 foot soldiers,

120 crossbowmen and harquebusiers, and 90 horseman. Cortés divided them into three armies that assaulted the city from three directions while the ships, loaded with cannons and landing forces, moved in on the lakes. What insured the Aztec defeat, however, was the fact that 90 percent of the attacking forces were experienced warriors from Tlaxcala and other city-states. The final battles were as much a native civil war against the Aztecs as a Spanish conquest.

The populace of the city was in weakened physical and spiritual condition when the three-month siege began. The Spaniards not only halted fresh water, food supplies, and transportation into the city with the brigantines, but they also attacked at every chance with their cannons and catapults to further weaken the capital. Initially, the Aztecs repulsed the multidirectional attacks with heavy losses to the invaders, and vicious fighting on the lakes and along the causeways continued as tactics shifted on both sides. In a scene symbolic of the shifting military advantage, the Spanish and Tlaxcalan warriors entered the ceremonial center near the Great Temple of Tenochtitlan, cut down Aztec warriors, and dragged one of their cannons to the top of the huge round stone used for sacrificing enemy warriors. They fired repeatedly at the Great Temple, while the priests beat their war drums incessantly until Spanish soldiers climbed up, cut the priests to pieces, and tossed their bodies over the sides. When counterattacked, the Spaniards fled and left the cannon behind. It was captured by the Aztecs, who pushed it into the lake so that it could not be used again. Hand-to-hand combat turned into utter mayhem in many parts of the city as the Aztecs were slowly pushed back; they lost control of neighborhoods, walkways, and canals until they made a last stand near the imperial marketplace at Tlatelolco where the brigantines could not penetrate.

Rape, murder, and dismemberment turned Tenochtitlan into a killing field until the Spaniards cornered the final Aztec *tlatoani* Cuauhtemoc (Diving Eagle) and his surviving troops in Tlatelolco.

There, Cuauhtemoc surrendered to Cortés thus ending the resistance of the Aztecs and signaling the fall of the capital city to the invaders. The date was August 13, 1521. The Spaniards and their Indian allies went on a rampage, plundering homes and palaces, and massacring thousands. Women were brutally raped and men were branded, beaten, and forced into servitude.

This haunting passage from the *Florentine Codex* marks our farewell to the Aztec capital:

> For their part, the men of Castile were searching for people along the roads. They were looking for gold. Jade, quetzal plumage, and turquoise had no importance for them. Women carried it in their breasts, under their petticoats, and the men, we carried it in our mouths or in our *maxtli* [loincloths]. And also they selected among the women those with dark skins, those with dark-skinned bodies. And some during the plunder covered their faces with mud and put on ragged clothes, tattered blouses. Everything which they wore was in shreds....All covered their noses with white handkerchiefs; they were nauseated by the dead bodies, already disintegrating.

The last Aztec ruler, Cuauhtemoc, was later tortured and hanged by Cortés, and the lineage of the powerful royal family reaching back to Acamapichtli came to a tragic end, one that still haunts Mexico and Spain. But at the site of Tlatelolco today there is a monument that announces a new beginning:

> On August 13, 1521, heroically defended by Cuauhtemoc, Tlatelolco fell to the power of Cortés. It was neither a triumph nor a defeat. It was the painful birth of the Mestizo people which is Mexico today.

Chapter 8
The return of the Aztecs

In Bernardino de Sahagún's account of Cortés's arrival on the coast of Mesoamerica we read that Motecuhzoma thought that "this was Topiltzin Quetzalcoatl who had come to land." The Aztec *tlatoani* was following an indigenous belief that the great Toltec man-god had prophesied that he would return one day to take up his throne and restore his fabled kingdom of Tollan. This account, told to Sahagún by native informants, has resulted in endless debates about whether the identification of Cortés with Quetzalcoatl returning to rule Mexico was fabricated by Spaniards years later or actually believed, for some months, by Motecuhzoma's royal court.

Today in Mexico and among some Latinos in the United States, there is still talk that Quetzalcoatl and other Aztec deities or heroes may return one day in some powerful symbolic and political form. One major reason for ongoing encounters with Aztecs is the repeated discoveries by Mexican archaeologists of Mexica monuments, buildings, and ritual objects. Today in Mexico more than one million people still speak Nahuatl, retell some of the ancient stories, and carry out some of the native ritual healing practices. Mexicans generally feel a deep pride in Aztec culture, and those living in Central Mexico inevitably encounter the Aztecs in archaeological zones, in world-class museums, and in their school curricula.

Aztecs in the colony

When the archaeologist Thomas Charlton examined colonial remains during an excavation in the Teotihuacan Valley, he discovered that traditional Aztec-style ceramics continued to be produced by native peoples well into the seventeenth century. In spite of the physical destruction, diseases, and religious conversions that assaulted native peoples, their craft-production techniques and numerous daily life activities continued even as the Spaniards took control. Charlton's work, along with that of Michael Smith and Elizabeth Brumfiel, have also shown the importance of looking beyond the ceremonial city of Tenochtitlan and into the everyday life of many productive rural communities in order to understand the Aztec world. One of the many benefits of this archaeological work, besides new insights into the lives of women, material culture, social organization, and center-periphery political relations during the Aztec empire, is the significant archaeological evidence of colonial Indian life. Many native communities, in continuing to produce Aztec-style objects, were not merely carrying on traditions of a lost past but rather were seeking ways of building their own political influence and economic resources, and exerting some control over their own lives. For instance, when Spaniards introduced their metal weapons and domestic implements into Mexico, the people of Xaltocan largely rejected them and instead actually increased their previous practice of mining obsidian and producing obsidian tools, advanced their productivity, and improved their economic conditions.

Unlike the Aztecs who appropriated the gods of peoples they dominated, Christian priests and laypeople did all they could to root out and destroy the rites, beliefs, and religious iconography of Mesoamerica. But the insistent friars themselves were forced to make adaptations and compromises when instructing natives on Christian beliefs in the Nahuatl language, which often resulted in new meanings given to notions of sin, crucifixion, sacrifice, salvation, saints, and God. Mesoamericans were resistant to entering the new churches, so architects created open chapels to allow growing numbers of Indians to attend outside masses and sermons. Native peoples did not merely acculturate to Spanish Catholicism, they combined elements of indigenous and Spanish culture and religion, picking and choosing from various traditions in order to meet their spiritual and physical needs in the changing society. Consider the various early colonial sculptures that combined Christian and Aztec imagery such as the baptismal font in Zinacantepec where images of Christ and Mary combine with symbols of the rain god Tlaloc. This kind of inventiveness took place in myriad forms of cultural mixing during the colonial period in Mesoamerica. One example vividly portrayed during the Mexican wars of independence from Spain at the beginning of the nineteenth century is that of Father José María Morelos. He was one of the spiritual and military leaders of the independence movements who invoked a line of Aztec heroes and the Spanish massacre in the sacred precinct of Tenochtitlan before the Noche Triste as models and justification for the rebellion against Spaniards, saying, "Spirits of Motecuhzoma, of Cacamatzin, of Cuauhtimotzin, of Xicotencatl and Catzonzi, celebrate, as you celebrated the *mitote* dance in which you were overcome by the treachery of Alvarado, this happy instant in which your children have come together to avenge the injustices and outrages."

Another example of the persistence of indigenous symbolic meanings into the colonial and modern eras is found in a few *cristos de caña*, papier-mâché figures of the crucified Christ made out of maize, the most sacred indigenous plant, inside of which were hidden colonial period manuscripts tallying onerous tribute payments. When native artists made these images of the crucified Jesus out of their revered corn plants, they were linking the profound knowledge they had of the divine seeds in plants with the new knowledge they had of the divine life inside of Christ.

The most powerful and pervasive example of mixing Aztec and Spanish religious elements is found in the apparitions of the Virgin of Guadalupe at a hill, associated with an Aztec goddess, outside the capital of New Spain in the early colonial period. Native, Mestizo, and Creole peoples adopted her as their own patron divinity, noting that she spoke Nahuatl during her apparitions, was dark-skinned like themselves, and offered them compassion while making ritual demands on the Spaniards. Everywhere one goes today in Mexican communities throughout the world you will find statues, images, and devotional practices in honor of this most sacred Mother of Mexico.

Aztec presences in Mexico today

In the last century, Mexican painters, composers, writers, and many other artists rediscovered indigenous cultures and incorporated their symbols, myths, and styles into their works. Many of the murals of Diego Rivera and José Clemente Orozco, the paintings of Frida Kahlo, as well as Mexican currency, novels, and dances incorporate Mesoamerican faces, practices, gods, and motifs. Every few years these creative works of art are periodically stimulated by the sensational discoveries in downtown Mexico City of Aztec stones, offerings caches, and ritual structures. When the excavation of the Great Aztec Temple was going on intensively from 1978 to 1983, the heightened media coverage led to millions of dinner conversations about the most recent finds. The director of this excavation, ironically named Eduardo Matos Moctezuma, has become a national hero, and millions of people from Mexico and around the world visit the excellent museum at the site. Every celebrity and head of state to visit Mexico is escorted to the excavation to view the Aztec wonders re-emerging from beneath Mexico City's surfaces. At the massive National Museum of Anthropology and History across the city in Chapultepec Park, Mexico's pre-Hispanic past is displayed in spacious rooms packed with colorful masterpieces in wood, stone, feathers, and other media. Significantly, the entire museum is anchored by the Mexica

Hall as if to say that Tenochtitlan and the mighty Aztecs are the lynchpin to this history. Placed in the middle of this huge room as though on a religious altar sits the great Sun Stone that shows the visitor that the Mexico of yesterday and today is a place of sun gods, calendars, and renewal.

The Nahuatl language flows through place names such as Coyoacan, Tepeyac, Tlatelolco, Chapultepec, Churubusco, and countless others. The Mexican Spanish lexicon contains more than three thousand "Nahuatlisms," and a number of English words come from Nahuatl including *tomato* from *tomatl*, *coyote* from *coyotl*, *mole* from *molli*, *tamale* from *tamalli*, *cuate* from *coatl* meaning both twin and serpent, and *chocolate* from *chocolatl*.

Today, when visiting the Zócalo, the great central square of Mexico City, one will see and hear energetic dancing, drumming, and chanting by representatives of an international movement of performers known as Danzantes. These feathered dancers stamp out Aztec foot rhythms to the sounds of conch shell trumpets, wooden drums, and ceramic whistles amid swirls of copal incense. Caught up in the spirit of the New Age, these dancers often deny that human sacrifice ever took place and believe that the pyramids are power spots linking them to the ghosts of the great *tlatoani* lords of Aztec Mexico. This movement has spread into many communities in the United States, and the Danzantes carry out their ritual practices in many cities while claiming that they have returned to Aztlan.

Since 2000, the Aztec story has attracted worldwide interest as evidenced in major museum exhibitions in Rome, New York City's Guggenheim Museum, the British Museum in London, the Getty Museum in Los Angeles, and the Field Museum in Chicago. The best-attended exhibition took place in Denver's Museum of Natural History in 1992 when nearly 800,000 people came to see a massive show called "Aztec: The World of Moctezuma."

Aztec moments and the return of Aztlan

When I was thirteen years old I had what I call my first "Aztec moment," a moment when I realized that to inherit the complexity and depth of Mexican history meant acknowledging some lineage to the Aztecs as well as the Spaniards. I also realized that the Aztecs were worth studying. My Aunt Milena took me to the old anthropology museum in downtown Mexico City, and I saw the Sun Stone, the great statue of Coatlicue, Maya jades, painted codices, sacrificial stones, and other fabulous cultural artifacts of ancient Mexico. In the midst of the many rooms containing colorful, monumental, and delicate Aztec art I began to feel a strong discomfort, a wave of contradictory feelings. Leaving the building in confusion I walked out into the great Zócalo near the Metropolitan Cathedral, adjacent to where the Great Aztec Temple once stood. I slowly realized that I felt two powerful emotions struggling within me. On one side I realized that I had taken feelings of shame at my Mexican ancestry into the museum. I felt shame because in American schools I was taught that Mexican culture had curios while Roman culture had empires; Aztecs made sacrifices while Greeks did philosophy; "Montezuma" caused "revenge" but the Egyptian pharaohs were geniuses. I had been taught to look down on the Aztecs and to look up to Old World civilizations. But a contradictory awareness surfaced as well. Looking around at the Metropolitan Cathedral and the National Palace, I realized that on these very places there once lived artists, philosophers, kings, and architects who designed, imagined, and made the cultural treasures I had just seen. All of this stimulated in me a great curiosity to learn all I could about the ancient civilizations of Mexico. And the longer I spent in Mexico City, the more I could see how the legacy of Aztec Mexico lives on in the foods, faces, words, symbols, and identities of contemporary Mexicans. These "Aztec moments" of awareness returned to me years later when I was a PhD student at the University of Chicago and chose to focus on religion in Mesoamerica.

I was not alone in this focus. Among many Chicanos and Latinos in the United States, Aztec place-names, stories, symbols, gods, and goddesses are actually growing in usage and representation. For example, the central political symbol of the Mexican American or Chicano civil rights movement of the 1960s and '70s was Aztlan, the fertile place of origin from which the Aztecs began their long, arduous journey to Tenochtitlan. Mexican Americans, perceiving they have been intentionally left out of the official cultural histories in the United States, have turned to indigenous and colonial Mexican culture for inspiration, stories, and symbols. At the National Chicano Youth Conference held in Denver in 1969, Chicano leaders read a political manifesto called "El Plan Espiritual de Aztlán" (The Spiritual Plan of Aztlan), which claimed that the American Southwest was the site of the original Aztlan, where the struggle for legal, territorial, and educational justice had to be carried out. Since then, many Mexican Americans, including student groups called MEChA (Movimiento Estudiantil Chicano de Aztlán), have embraced the symbol of Aztlan to express something integral to being Chicano. Cultural centers throughout the United States are covered with murals combining Aztlan symbolism with images of Aztec and Maya deities, and contemporary life in Latino communities. The leading Mexican American academic journal is called *Aztlán*. Recurring Aztec symbols in Latino/a art include the eagle and the serpent, La Malinche as a culture heroine, *calaveras* (skeletons) recalling Aztec skull racks (only now, representing the suffering of victims of violence), and Aztec goddesses. The blooming cactus theme is a sign that numerous Chicano artists support the struggle of Latin American farm workers and also value the indigenous plants in local cuisine and healing practices. The various images of Mesoamerican goddesses show that new assessments of contemporary women's experiences and powers are being explored. In these ways, Aztec beliefs in the powers of underground caves, bones, and seeds are revived by these modern-day keepers of the "red and black" who identify with the Mexica past.

12. A Day of the Dead altar in Mexico City.

To the pleasant surprise of many Latinos and non-Latinos alike, communities throughout the United States now include festive, emotional Día de los Muertos (Day of the Dead) celebrations around the time of Halloween. From Harvard University's Peabody Museum of Archaeology and Ethnology to San Diego State University, people construct colorful public altars honoring the recent and honored dead. Like the families who erect Day of the Dead altars in their homes, these public displays reflect both the Christian All Saints' Days and pre-Hispanic rituals dedicated to the ancestors. They are decorated with vibrant yellow or orange marigolds the Aztecs called *cempoalxochitl* (Twenty Flower, signifying the completion of a life), sugar skulls, food offerings, and photographs of the deceased. If you look closely at these altars you may notice a humorous, tender image of the Aztec spirit-dog Xolotl, standing on a pedestal by the underground river on the way to Mictlan, waiting to guide the souls of the dead to the other shore. These celebratory altars emphasize the Aztec image of death and regeneration rather than the contrary image of sacrifice and conquest. It seems that the spirits of Aztlan are starting out again on a journey to a new and hopeful world.

References

Chapter 1

Bernal Díaz del Castillo, *The History of the Conquest of New Spain*, ed. Davíd Carrasco (Albuquerque: University of New Mexico Press, 2008).

William T. Sanders, "Tenochtitlan in 1519: A Pre-Industrial Megalopolis," in *The Aztec World*, ed. Elizabeth M. Brumfiel and Gary M. Feinman, 67–85 (New York: Abrams, 2008).

William B. Taylor and Ken Mills, eds., *Colonial Spanish America: A Documentary History* (Wilmington, DE: Scholarly Resources, 1998).

Bernardino de Sahagún, *Florentine Codex: General History of the Things of New Spain*, ed. Arthur J. O. Anderson and Charles E. Dibble, introductory vol. and 12 books (Santa Fe, NM: School for American Research and University of Utah, 1950–82).

Eduardo Matos Moctezuma, "Templo Mayor: History and Interpretation," in Johanna Broda, Davíd Carrasco, and Eduardo Matos Moctezuma, *The Great Temple of Tenochtitlan: Center and Periphery in the Aztec World*, 15–60 (Berkeley: University of California Press, 1987).

Lewis Henry Morgan, "Montezuma's Dinner," *North American Review* 122 (1876): 265–308.

Miguel León-Portilla, *The Broken Spears: The Aztec Account of the Conquest of Mexico* (Boston: Beacon, 1990).

Chapter 2

Carlos Fuentes, *Where the Air Is Clear* (New York: Farrar, Straus, and Giroux, 1968).

Elizabeth Hill Boone, *Stories in Red and Black: Pictorial Histories of the Aztecs and Mixtecs* (Austin: University of Texas Press, 2008).

Dana Leibsohn, "Codex Aubin," in *The Oxford Encyclopedia of Mesoamerican Cultures*, ed. Davíd Carrasco, 3 vols., 1:60–61 (New York: Oxford University Press, 2001).

Diego Durán, *The History of the Indies of New Spain*, ed. Doris Heyden (Norman: University of Oklahoma Press, 1994).

Hernando Alvarado Tezozómoc, *Crónica mexicayotl* (Mexico City: Universidad Nacional Autónoma de México, 1998).

Felipe Solís, "The Art of the Aztec Era," in *The Aztec World*, ed. Elizabeth M. Brumfiel and Gary Feinman, 153–77 (New York: Abrams, 2009).

Bernardino de Sahagún, *Florentine Codex: General History of the Things of New Spain*, ed. Arthur J. O. Anderson and Charles E. Dibble, introductory vol. and 12 books (Santa Fe, NM: School for American Research and University of Utah, 1950–82), book 7.

René Millon, ed., *Urbanization at Teotihuacan, Mexico*, 3 vols. (Austin: University of Texas Press, 1973).

Esther Pasztory, *Teotihuacan: An Experiment in Living* (Norman: University of Oklahoma Press, 1997).

Bernardino de Sahagún, *Florentine Codex*, books 3 and 10.

Alba Guadalupe Mastache, Robert H. Cobean, and Dan M. Healan, *Ancient Tollan: Tula and the Toltec Heartland* (Boulder: University Press of Colorado, 2002).

James M. Adovasio and David Pedler, "The Peopling of North America," in *North American Archaeology*, ed. Timothy R. Pauketat and Diana DiPaolo Loren, 30–55 (Malden, MA: Blackwell, 2005).

Chapter 3

Frances F. Berdan and Patricia Rieff Anawalt, *The Essential Codex Mendoza* (Berkeley: University of California Press, 1996).

Jeffrey Parsons, "Environment and Rural Economy," in *The Aztec World*, ed. Elizabeth M. Brumfiel and Gary M. Feinman, 23–52 (New York: Abrams, 2008).

Susan D. Gillespie, *The Aztec Kings: The Construction of Rulership in Mexican History* (Tucson: University of Arizona Press, 1992).

Ross Hassig, *Aztec Warfare: Imperial Expansion and Political Control* (Norman: University of Oklahoma, 1995).

Warwick Bray, *Everyday Life of the Aztecs* (New York: Peter Bedrick, 1991).

Karl Taube, *Aztec and Maya Myths* (Austin: University of Texas Press, 1997).

Anthony Aveni, *Skywatchers: A Revised and Updated Version of Skywatchers of Ancient Mexico* (Austin: University of Texas Press, 2001).

Chapter 4

Leonardo López Luján, *Offerings of the Templo Mayor of Tenochtitlan* (Albuquerque: University of New Mexico Press, 2005).

Alfredo López Austin, *Human Body and Ideology: Concepts of the Ancient Nahuas* (Salt Lake City: University of Utah Press, 1988).

Henry B. Nicholson, "The New Tenochtitlan Templo Mayor Coyolxauhqui-Chantico Monument," *Indiana (Gedenkschrift Gerdt Kutscher*, Teil 2) 10 (1985): 77–98.

Alfredo López Austin and Leonardo López Luján, "Aztec Human Sacrifice," in *The Aztec World*, ed. Elizabeth M. Brumfiel and Gary M. Feinman, 137–52 (New York: Abrams, 2008).

Bernardino de Sahagún, *Florentine Codex: General History of the Things of New Spain*, ed. Arthur J. O. Anderson and Charles E. Dibble, introductory vol. and 12 books (Santa Fe, NM: School for American Research and University of Utah, 1950–82), book 2.

Michael Harner, "The Ecological Basis for Aztec Sacrifice," *American Ethnologist* 4 (1977): 117–35.

Marvin Harris, *Cannibals and Kings: The Origins of Culture* (New York: Vintage, 1991).

Bernard Ortiz de Montellano, "Counting Skulls: Comment on the Cannibalism Theory of Harner-Harris," *American Anthropologist* 85 (1983): 403–6.

David Carrasco, *City of Sacrifice: Violence from the Aztec Empire to the Modern Americas* (Boston: Beacon Books, 2000).

Chapter 5

Elizabeth Brumfiel, "Aztec Women: Capable Partners and Cosmic Enemies," in *The Aztec World*, ed. Elizabeth M. Brumfiel and Gary M. Feinman, 87–104 (New York: Abrams, 2008).

Cecelia F. Klein, "Rethinking Cihuacoatl: Aztec Political Imagery of the Conquered Woman," in *Smoke and Mist: Mesoamerican Studies in Memory of Thelma D. Sullivan*, ed. J. Kathryn Josserand and Karen Dakin, 237–77 (Oxford: British Archaeological Reports, International Series 404, 1988).

June Nash, "The Aztecs and the Ideology of Male Dominance," *Signs* 4 (1978): 349–62.

Bernard Ortiz de Montellano, *Aztec Medicine, Health, and Nutrition* (New Brunswick, NJ: Rutgers University Press, 1990).

Chapter 6

Miguel León-Portilla, *The Aztec Image of Self and Society: An Introduction to Nahua Culture* (Salt Lake City: University of Utah Press, 1992).

Bernardino de Sahagún, *Florentine Codex: General History of the Things of New Spain*, ed. Arthur J. O. Anderson and Charles E. Dibble, introductory vol. and 12 books (Santa Fe, NM: School for American Research and University of Utah, 1950–82), book 6.

Elizabeth Boone, *Stories in Red and Black: Pictorial Histories of the Aztecs and Mixtecs* (Austin: University of Texas Press, 2000).

Davíd Carrasco and Scott Sessions, eds., *Cave, City, and Eagle's Nest: An Interpretive Journey through the Mapa de Cuauhtinchan No. 2* (Albuquerque: University of New Mexico Press , 2007).

Eduardo Matos Moctezuma and Leonardo López Luján, *Monumental Mexica Sculpture* (Mexico City: Fundación Conmemoraciones, 2010).

Chapter 7

Bernal Díaz del Castillo, *The History of the Conquest of New Spain*, ed. Davíd Carrasco (Albuquerque: University of New Mexico Press, 2008).

Sandra Messinger Cypess, "La Malinche as Palimpsest II," in Díaz del Castillo, *History of the Conquest of New Spain*, 418–38.

Miguel León-Portilla, *The Broken Spears: The Aztec Account of the Conquest of Mexico* (Boston: Beacon, 1990).

Hernán Cortés, *Letters from Mexico*, ed. Anthony Pagden (New Haven, CT: Yale University Press, 2001).

Ross Hassig, *Mexico and the Spanish Conquest* (Norman: University of Oklahoma Press, 2006).

Chapter 8

Thomas Charlton, Cynthia L. Otis Charlton, and Patricia Fournier García, "The Basin of Mexico AD 1450–1620: Archaeological Dimensions," in *The Postclassic to Spanish-Era Transition in*

Mesoamerica: Archaeological Perspectives, ed. Susan Kepecs and Rani T. Alexander, 49–63 (Albuquerque: University of New Mexico Press, 2005).

Michael E. Smith, *Aztecs* (Malden, MA: Blackwell, 2003).

Elizabeth Brumfiel, "Aztec Women: Capable Partners and Cosmic Enemies," in *The Aztec World*, ed. Elizabeth M. Brumfiel and Gary M. Feinman, 87–104 (New York: Abrams, 2008).

Louise Burkhart, *The Slippery Earth: Nahua-Christian Moral Dialogue in Sixteenth-Century Mexico* (Tucson: University of Arizona Press, 1989).

Luis Laso de la Vega, *The Story of Guadalupe: Luis Laso de la Vega's Huei tlamahuiçoltica of 1649*, ed. Lisa Sousa, Stafford Poole, and James Lockhart (Stanford, CA: Stanford University Press; Los Angeles: UCLA Latin American Center Publications, 1998).

Guillermo Bonfil Batalla, *México Profundo: Reclaiming a Civilization* (Austin: University of Texas Press, 1996).

Elizabeth Carmichael and Chloë Sayer, *The Skeleton at the Feast: The Day of the Dead in Mexico* (Austin: University of Texas Press, 1992).

Further reading

Chapter 1

There are several good introductions to the symbolism and archaeology of the Great Aztec Temple, including Eduardo Matos Moctezuma, *Life and Death in the Templo Mayor* (Niwot: University Press of Colorado, 1995); Leonardo López Luján, *Offerings of the Templo Mayor of Tenochtitlan*, rev. ed. (Albuquerque: University of New Mexico Press, 2005); and Johanna Broda, Davíd Carrasco, and Eduardo Matos Moctezuma, *The Great Temple of Tenochtitlan: Center and Periphery in the Aztec World* (Berkeley: University of California Press, 1989), especially Broda's views on Aztec cosmovision and ritual. For other aspects of Aztec life and society, see the excellent essays, including Michael E. Smith's cogent "The Aztec Empire" (121–36), in *The Aztec World* (New York: Abrams, 2008), an exhibition catalogue for the Field Museum in Chicago, edited by Elizabeth M. Brumfiel and Gary M. Feinman. To understand the distinctive contributions of Mesoamerican peoples in making the first cities in the Americas in comparative perspective, see Paul Wheatley's magisterial *The Pivot of the Four Quarters: A Preliminary Enquiry into the Origins and Character of the Ancient Chinese City* (Chicago: Aldine, 1971). On the many historical problems of understanding what went on in Central Mexico during the Spanish invasion, see Matthew Restall, *Seven Myths of the Spanish Conquest* (New York: Oxford University Press, 2004).

Chapter 2

A well-written and up-to-date overview of Aztec origins appears
in Richard Townsend, *The Aztecs* (London: Thames and Hudson,
2009). A new interpretation of the myth of Aztlan appears in chap. 5
("Aztec Moments and Chicano Cosmovision: Aztlan Recalled to Life")
of Eduardo Matos Moctezuma and Davíd Carrasco, *Moctezuma's
Mexico: Visions of the Aztec World*, rev. ed. (Niwot: University Press
of Colorado, 2003). For a focused discussion of recent discoveries of
military might and ritual violence at Teotihuacan, see Saburo Sugiyama,
*Human Sacrifice, Militarism, and Rulership: Materialization of State
Ideology at the Feathered Serpent Pyramid, Teotihuacan* (Cambridge:
Cambridge University Press, 2005). The finest historical analysis of
the Feathered Serpent cult that influenced Aztec society is Henry
B. Nicholson, *Topiltzin Quetzalcoatl: The Once and Future Lord of the
Toltecs* (Boulder: University Press of Colorado, 2001). Maarten Jansen
and Gabina Aurora Pérez Jiménez, *Encounter with the Plumed Serpent:
Drama and Power in the Heart of Mesoamerica* (Boulder: University
Press of Colorado, 2007), provides a wider view of the Feathered
Serpent's impact beyond the Basin of Mexico. Cholula's deep historical
significance as a great religious capital is discussed in Geoffrey G.
McCafferty, "Tollan Chollan and the Legacy of Legitimacy during the
Classic–Postclassic Transition," in *Mesoamerica's Classic Heritage: From
Teotihuacan to the Aztecs*, ed. Davíd Carrasco, Lindsay Jones, and Scott
Sessions, 341–67 (Boulder: University Press of Colorado, 1999).

Chapter 3

Frances F. Berdan and Patricia Rieff Anawalt's handsome four-volume
edition of *The Codex Mendoza* (Berkeley: University of California Press,
1992) includes a full-color facsimile and comprehensive interpretative
analyses from leading scholars. The most thorough analysis of the
New Fire Ceremony appears in Johanna Broda, "La fiesta azteca del
Fuego Nuevo y el culto de las Pleiades," in *Space and Time in the
Cosmovision of Mesoamerica*, ed. Franz Tichy, 129–58 (Munich: Fink,
1982). A valuable overview of agricultural practices is found in Teresa
Rojas Rabiela, "Agriculture" and "Chinampa Agriculture," in *The
Oxford Encyclopedia of Mesoamerican Cultures*, ed. Davíd Carrasco,
3 vols., 1:3–8, 200–201 (New York: Oxford University Press, 2001).
The rise and fall of Aztec kings are mapped out in three important
studies: Nigel Davies, *The Aztecs* (London: Folio Society, 2000);

Michael E. Smith, *The Aztecs* (Malden, MA: Blackwell, 2003); and the most detailed reconstruction: Susan Gillespie, *The Aztec Kings: The Construction of Rulership in Mexican History* (Tucson: University of Arizona Press, 1989). The troubled life of Motecuhzoma is examined in Michel Graulich, *Montezuma, ou, L'apogée et la chute de l'empire aztèque* (Paris: Fayard, 1994). Recent scholarship on the tribute empire of the Aztecs is summarized in Deborah L. Nichols, "Artisans, Markets, and Merchants," in *The Aztec World*, ed. Elizabeth M. Brumfiel and Gary M. Feinman, 105–20 (New York: Abrams, 2008). Access to the worldview of the Aztecs is found in Anthony Aveni, *Skywatchers: A Revised and Updated Version of Skywatchers of Ancient Mexico* (Austin: University of Texas Press, 2001).

Chapter 4

The best recent scholarship on the practice of ritual sacrifice appears in Leonardo López Lujan and Guilhem Olivier, eds., *El sacrificio humano en la tradición religiosa mesoamericana* (Mexico City: INAH and UNAM, 2010), containing articles interpreting the ritual killing of humans across Mesoamerican history and geography. Eduardo Matos Moctezuma, *La muerte entre los mexicas* (Mexico City: Tusquets, 2010), explores the meaning of death and death rituals in the Aztec city. An excellent overview relating the psychology of violence and the ceremonial traditions of sacrifice is found in Yólotl González Torres, *El sacrificio humano entre los mexicas* (Mexico City: Fondo de Cultura Económica, 2006). Inga Clendinnen, *Aztecs: An Interpretation* (Cambridge: Cambridge University Press, 1995), is an elegantly written account of the ways sacrifice was interwoven with daily life, aesthetics, and religious worldview in Tenochtitlan. For an interpretive overview of the sacrifice of warriors, women, and children as well as cannibalism see Davíd Carrasco, *City of Sacrifice: Violence from the Aztec Empire to the Modern Americas* (Boston: Beacon Books, 2000).

Chapter 5

Scholarship on the role of women in the Aztec world and beyond is summarized in Cecelia Klein, "Gender Studies," *The Oxford Encyclopedia of Mesoamerican Cultures,* ed. Davíd Carrasco, 3 vols., 1:435–38 (New York: Oxford University Press, 2001). Susan Kellogg, "From Parallel and Equivalent to Separate but Unequal: Tenochca Mexica Women, 1500–1700," in *Indian Women of Early*

Mexico, ed. Susan Schroeder, Stephanie Wood, and Robert Haskett, 121–43 (Norman: University of Oklahoma Press, 1997), examines the changing roles and status of indigenous women in the transition from Tenochtitlan to Mexico City. Karen Vieira Powers, *Women in the Crucible of Conquest: The Gendered Genesis of Spanish American Society, 1500–1600* (Albuquerque: University of New Mexico, 2005), provides a cultural understanding of the tremendous challenges facing females in early colonial Mexican society. Louise Burkhart shows how Aztec women's work in the home had religious dimensions in "Mexica Women on the Home Front: Housework and Religion in Aztec Mexico," in Schroeder, Wood, and Haskett, *Indian Women of Early Mexico*, 25–54. Children have recently received new attention in Traci Ardren and Scott R. Hutson, eds., *The Social Experience of Childhood in Ancient Mesoamerica* (Boulder: University Press of Colorado, 2006).

Chapter 6

The aesthetic world of the Aztecs is creatively surveyed in part 3 ("The Sacred") of Inga Clendinnen, *Aztecs: An Interpretation* (Cambridge: Cambridge University Press, 1991), 211–63. Guilhem Olivier, *Mockeries and Metamorphoses of an Aztec God: Tezcatlipoca, Lord of the Smoking Mirror* (Boulder: University Press of Colorado, 2003), explores the Aztec delight in metaphors and dualities. Gary Tomlinson, *The Singing of the New World: Indigenous Voice in the Era of European Contact* (Cambridge: Cambridge University Press, 2007), adeptly works through colonial sources to recover the Aztec voice in poetry and song. An innovative scholarly study of Nahua poetry appears in Jongsoo Lee, *The Allure of Nezahualcoyotl: Pre-Hispanic History, Religion, and Nahua Poetics* (Albuquerque: University of New Mexico Press, 2008). The traditions and innovations on various forms of writing in Central Mexico are skillfully surveyed in Dana Leibsohn, *Script and Glyph: Pre-Hispanic History, Colonial Bookmaking, and the Historia Tolteca-Chichimeca* (Washington, DC: Dumbarton Oaks, 2009).

Chapter 7

The most thorough historical summary of the fall of the Aztecs appears in Ross Hassig, *Mexico and the Spanish Conquest* (Norman:

University of Oklahoma Press, 2006). Also see Serge Gruzinski, *Aztecs: Rise and Fall of an Empire* (New York: Abrams; London: Thames and Hudson, 1992), for a dramatic rendering of this epic story. For Aztec accounts of the encounter between Spaniards and native Mesoamerican communities, see Miguel León-Portilla, *The Broken Spears: The Aztec Account of the Conquest of Mexico* (Boston: Beacon, 1990), and James Lockhart, *We People Here: Nahuatl Accounts of the Conquest of Mexico* (Berkeley: University of California Press, 1993). The best critical reading of a Spanish account of the conquest can be found in Cristián Roa de la Carrera, *Histories of Infamy: Francisco López de Gómara and the Ethics of Spanish Imperialism* (Boulder: University Press of Colorado, 2005), which deconstructs the biases and literary strategies of Cortés's secretary. Interest in the Aztecs has gone beyond the field of historical writing to the work of novelists, poets, and cultural mythmakers. A number of novels about the role of Malinche have appeared in recent years including the work by the Mexican author, Laura Esquivel, *Malinche: A Novel* (New York: Atria, 2006). Gary Jennings, *Aztec* (New York: Atheneum, 1980; repr. New York: Forge, 2007), is by far the most widely read novel about any Mesoamerican society and is based on widespread research and the author's vivid imagination.

Chapter 8

The best introduction to the many ways the story of Aztlan continues to influence scholarship and art is Virginia M. Fields and Victor Zamudio-Taylor, eds., *The Road to Aztlan: Art from a Mythic Homeland* (Los Angeles: Los Angeles County Museum of Art, 2001). Guillermo Bonfil Batalla, *México Profundo: Reclaiming a Civilization* (Austin: University of Texas Press, 1996), continues to inspire new thinking about the persistence and change of Aztec and other Mesoamerican cultural practices today. The best ethnographic and pictorial presentation of Day of the Dead rituals appears in Elizabeth Carmichael and Chloë Sayer, *The Skeleton at the Feast: The Day of the Dead in Mexico* (Austin: University of Texas Press, 1992). John Phillip Santos, *Places Left Unfinished at the Time of Creation* (New York: Penguin, 2000), is a memoir that beautifully illustrates how contemporary Latinos, especially in Texas, link the Latino present to the imaginary worlds of their ancestors, enabling new formulations of cultural identity. Gloria Anzaldúa, *Borderlands = La Frontera: The*

New Mestiza (San Francisco: Aunt Lute, 1987), has become a literary and spiritual guide for Latino readers and draws directly on Aztec myths and images. Cherríe Moraga, *A Xicana Codex of Changing Consciousness: Writings, 2000–2010* (Durham, NC: Duke University Press, 2011), draws on the messages and meanings of Mesoamerican codices to illuminate contemporary struggles for creativity among Chicana/o feminists, queers, and indigenous activists.

Index